LIFE AMONGST
THE TROUBRIDGES

To the four without whose help
there would be no book

CYNTHIA
DIANA
MARIE-JAQUELINE
FELIX

LIFE AMONGST
THE TROUBRIDGES

by Laura Troubridge

JOURNALS OF A YOUNG VICTORIAN
1873-1884

Edited By

Jaqueline Hope-Nicholson

TITE STREET PRESS

This revised edition with additional illustrations
first published in 1999 by Tite Street Press,
42a Palace Gardens Terrace, London W8 4RR

Copyright © 1999 by Jean Baptiste Hugo for the estate of Laura
[Troubridge] Hope
Editing and annotations copyright © 1999 by
Marie-Jaqueline Lancaster

Distributed by Gazelle Book Services Limited
Falcon House, Queen Square
Lancaster, England LA1 1RN

First published by John Murray, 1966
Copyright © by Jaqueline Hope-Nicholson

British Library Cataloguing in Publication Data
A catalogue record for this book is available from the British
Library

ISBN 0 9534746 0 7

This publication is managed by Amolibros, Watchet, Somerset
Printed and bound by Professional Book Supplies, Oxford,
England

Contents

Illustrations

TROUBRIDGE FAMILY TREE

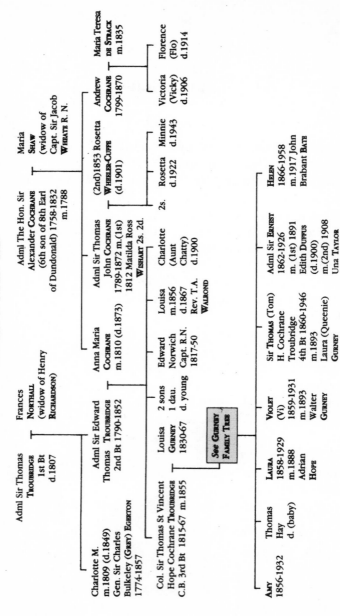

NOTE *Not all members of large families are included here*

GURNEY FAMILY TREE

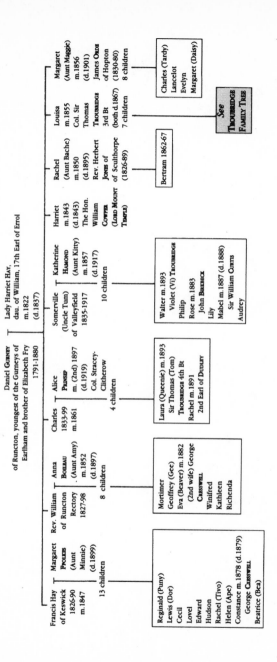

NOTE *Not all members of large families are included here*

Introduction
to the First Edition

For a long time I have wanted to compile from her papers an account of my mother, Laura Troubridge, later Mrs Adrian Hope, the pastelist, for she was a delightful and unusual person. Although she was born in 1858 her upbringing from the age of nine (when she and her brothers and sisters became orphans) was really that of a former generation as they lived with their maternal grandfather in Norfolk. He was very old-fashioned, and had changed nothing since the death of his wife in the 1830s, so this account of their early life forms something of a period piece.

I have drawn from two sources of material, the journals my mother wrote from the age of fifteen, very detailed and naive, with the violent prejudices of youth; and the memoirs of her family and childhood written afterwards. As these two threads are necessarily interwoven in the first part of the book, I have added chapter headings to explain transitions from one source to another. It was the diaries of Grandfather Daniel Gurney's sisters, including those of Elizabeth Fry (known to the family as Aunt Fry) which inspired Laura Troubridge to write her journals.

Jaqueline Hope-Nicholson
More House, Tite Street, Chelsea, 1966

Foreword

My late mother Jaqueline Hope-Nicholson was often asked by her readers what happened to 'Laura and Adrian' after their engagement in 1884 when this book ends. As Laura's younger granddaughter I have had the great pleasure of reading the daily letters Laura and Adrian exchanged during their four-year engagement until their marriage in 1888.

This correspondence provides a fascinating account of the times from totally different points of view. Adrian has been appointed Secretary and Fundraiser to the Great Ormond Street Hospital for Sick Children. He manages to combine this badly-paid and sometimes onerous work with a highly active social life, curbed by the ever-present problems of his unstable father whose sole interest lies with his, as yet, unprofitable 'Hope Gun' project. Adrian amuses Laura with his witty descriptions of London Life, especially the demeanour and appearance of the ladies, but these are interspersed with expessions of his heartfelt agony at lacking sufficient funds with which to set up house in style with Laura. Neither of them would consider starting off married life from a set of modest rooms. As it is, they do not find the Studio house of their dreams - More House in Tite Street, Chelsea - until 1892, well into their married life.

In contrast, Laura is tied to the little house in Hunstanton that she shares with her four sisters, with occasional forays to London when she often manages to elude the worst confines of chaperonage. She has a sharp eye for the absurd and transforms her daily round into a series of hilarious anecdotes, mostly recounting the country house visits to her endless relations: the Barclays, Birkbecks, Boileaus, Buxtons, Cochranes, Gurneys galore, Leghs, O'Neils, St Aubyns, and many more.

She continues drawing, illustrating, and painting pastel portraits while longing for professional teaching. Nevertheless, her work is praised by such artists as Sir John Millais, Sargent, Randolph Caldecott, Lewis Carroll, Kate Greenaway, and the great Oscar Wilde himself of whose elder son she does a charming pastel portrait. Between times she writes and produces amateur theatricals in which she plays the lead (to great acclaim), there being no other born actress in her somewhat restricted circle.

I am preparing this sequel to *Life Amongst the Troubridges* for publication as: *Letters of Engagement - the Love Letters of Adrian Hope and Laura Troubridge, 1884-1888*

Marie-Jaqueline Lancaster
Tite Street Press, London, 1998

My Parents

My father, Colonel Sir Thomas Troubridge, was a distinguished soldier, a brave man who, fighting in the Crimea as a young bachelor, won many medals and honours which he paid for with much that makes for happiness in this life. A tall, strong, active man, fond of sport and travel, he was terribly wounded in 1854 at the battle of Inkerman and had to have one leg and the other foot amputated.

The letter he wrote to his sister Louisa, telling them at home what had befallen him, shows far better than I could the brave, unselfish spirit that was his. All his thought was for them, to break the news gently to those he loved – his widowed mother and two sisters (Lady Troubridge, *née* Anna Maria Cochrane, Louisa and Chatty). There is no word of himself or of the future, which must have appeared dark and sorrowful. The letter is written the day after the battle of Inkerman:

Camp before Sebastopol – Nov. 6th 1854

My dear Louisa,

You will be sorry to hear that we have had another desperate engagement yesterday. The Grand Dukes Michael and Constantine have arrived with reinforcements, and, making first a false attack on Balaclava, they came up the hills from Sebastopol in great force. Our troops, being very much scattered in consequence of the extended position we were obliged to occupy, they got very close to our tents before the reserves could come up to our assistance. However we managed to hold our ground till the French came up and turned the enemy's flank – when, after about eight hours hard fighting, they retired, having suffered a loss of – it is said – from eight to ten thousand killed and wounded, while ours is put down at two thousand – but of course so soon after an action nothing positive can be known. Poor Sir G. Cathcart is killed and four or five generals are wounded.

I

Now, my dear Louisa, you must not be alarmed, as you see that I am able to write as usual, and, I assure you, that I am neither in pain nor yet in danger, but you will be sorry to hear that dear Chatty's predictions as to my escaping all dangers have not been verified. I was posted at the advance battery, where I was on the day of the former engagement, and we were exposed to a very heavy fire of every description. I was unfortunately struck by a large round shot on the right leg and left foot. I had presence of mind to lay down immediately and put my legs up in the air till a doctor could be found, so that I did not lose any blood, and he bandaged me up, and when the firing was nearly over I was carried back to the Camp. It was found necessary to perform two operations, which were done with great skill by Dr. Alexander, Staff Surgeon of the Brigade, under chloroform. I really did not know that I had been touched and did not suffer the least pain, either at the time of the accident or since. I have had a very good night and slept a good deal and have not the slightest fever. I hope you will all receive this intelligence with the same resignation with which I have been enabled to bear it. Two poor fellows were killed by the same shot. Having lost a leg and part of a foot I am not likely to be of much more use in the fighting line at present, and shall probably be sent down to Scutari shortly. I will let you know what I am advised by medical men to do — as of course for some time I shall be in their hands. Now I hope you will take this coolly as I do, and reflect how much worse it might have been. The doctors assure me I shall be able to hobble along very creditably and to ride — so when you write do not tell me that you are miserable about me and that sort of thing — as it will only worry me and I know exactly your feelings on the subject. Graham paid me a visit yesterday evening and seems to feel my accident more than I do myself. Pray give my best love to my mother and Chatty and tell them that I have every confidence that all this is for the best, as it has pleased God to visit me with affliction, it is my duty to bear it with resignation.

Believe me, my dear sister,
Your most affec. brother T. St. V. Troubridge.

Thus tenderly did he try to calm and comfort those three lone and sorrowful women, knowing the grief it would be to them to hear their only son and brother was crippled for life. He makes so light of his heroism on the day – but this is an account of an eye-witness:

'Sir Thomas being in command of a battery at Inkerman was wounded early in the day, by a shot from the round tower of Sebastopol. He behaved with great calm, in spite of the terrible nature of his wounds, telling the doctor to put on a tourniquet and to prop his shattered legs up against a gun carriage that he should not bleed to death. The doctor wished to carry him out of the fight, but Sir Thomas said, 'No – he should last out the day', and continued to give the order to fire in as unmoved a voice as he had before he was wounded. It was not till six o'clock, when the battle was won, that he was persuaded to leave the field and be carried back to the Camp – where the surgeons amputated his leg and foot.'

And this extract from a letter from Queen Victoria to Leopold, King of the Belgians, gives an idea of the sympathy for someone so wounded:

Buckingham Palace – May 22nd 1856

. . . Ernest [Duke of Saxe-Coburg Gotha, brother of the Prince Consort] *will have told you what a beautiful and touching sight and ceremony – (the first of the kind ever witnessed in England) the distribution of the Medals was. From the highest Prince of the Blood to the lowest Private all received the same distinction for the bravest conduct in the severest actions, and the rough hand of the brave and honest private soldier came for the first time in contact with that of their sovereign and their Queen! Noble fellows, I own I feel as if they were* my own children. *My heart beats for* them *as for my nearest and dearest. They were so touched – so pleased. Many I hear cried – and they won't hear of giving up their Medals, to have their names engraved upon them, for fear they should not receive the identical one put into* their hands by me, *which is quite touching. Several came by in a sadly mutilated state. None created more interest or is more gallant than young Sir Thomas Troubridge, who had, at Inkerman,*

one leg and the other foot carried away by a round shot, and continued commanding his battery till the battle was won. He was dragged by in a bath chair and, when I gave him his medal, I told him I should make him one of my Aides-de-Camp, for his very gallant conduct, to which he replied – 'I am amply repaid for everything.' One must revere and love such soldiers as these.

Sir Thomas was made a C.B. and given the rank of Brevet Colonel, he also received the Legion of Honour and the Medgidie [Turkish Crimean War medal]. He later had a good appointment at the Horse Guards as head of the Army Clothing Department, amongst other duties designing some uniforms of the date. Admiral Sir John Hay, a cousin, told me many years ago how he went on board the troopship to meet my father on his landing at Portsmouth from the Crimea: 'When I saw him lying on an invalid chair, a helpless wreck of the fine athletic man he had been – I thought to myself – poor Troubridge, why was he not killed outright – how far better for him . . . but I lived to see I was wrong. Your father made a happy marriage and, surrounded with wife and children he loved and doing work that interested him for many years – well, it was just another example that human judgements are often mistaken. No one meeting your father in his later years could fail to see his life was unusually happy in spite of all he had suffered in the Crimea.'

After a long convalescence at Scutari and Malta my father lived with his mother and sisters in their house in Eaton Place. One summer afternoon a certain Louisa Jane Gurney, who was young, beautiful, and greatly loved for her gentleness and charm, went out driving with her sister-in-law – Mrs. Willie Gurney – to call on her old friends Louisa and Chatty Troubridge at Eaton Place. The butler said, 'Not at home', but on looking at the cards they left, he added, 'If it is Miss Gurney, Sir Thomas particularly wants to see her.' This seemed rather strange and surprising, but no wish of the 'Hero of the Crimea' (as my father was often called) could be disregarded, and so she went to meet her Fate and sailed into the room where my father was sitting on a chair, a blue silk quilt hiding his maimed limbs, and with a kind smile on his face for the old, invalid lady he expected to see! For a certain Miss Anna Gurney, of Northrepps, had promised to call to show him a particular kind of chair she used in which she could wheel herself from room to room, and which it was proposed he should copy. But the gods sent him instead of the old lame cousin the beautiful woman who was to be to him the joy of his life. The mistake was soon explained and my father persuaded her to wait for his sisters' return. Mrs. Willie Gurney discreetly withdrew, leaving them together and promising to call in an hour. Thus they had the chance of a long tête-á-tête, unusual I fancy in those days of heavy chaperonage, for his two sisters failed to appear, and thus the romance of my parents began.

This is how my mother described the fateful meeting in her diary:

May 29th 1855

I have seen Sir T. Troubridge, who I was very anxious to become acquainted with. It was such an odd feeling being with him first. I expected him to be very pale and thin and suffering-looking, instead of which he is a large, strong man with a high colour and red moustache and beard. A blue quilt was over his legs, and as he sat in his chair, no one would have said that anything was the matter with him. He is perfectly cheerful and seemed in capital spirits. He must be very happy minded and deeply religious or he could not bear such an affliction as he does. He does not appear to wish much for sympathy, but rather shrinks from it. Louisa is quite devoted to her brother and lives only for him. I suppose he will marry though it would be a self-sacrificing person who would become the wife of a man so perfectly helpless. But I can imagine if a person loved him intensely (and he deserves to be loved) they would find a pleasure in doing so.

I think there were not many dragons in their path . . . for the following November they were married, at St. Michael's Church, Chester Square. My father was just able to walk by then, with his artificial leg and foot, and on crutches. And so they lived happily ever after, as the fairy stories say, but alas in their case not for very long. They were together for only twelve years.

Setting the Family Scene

I, Laura Troubridge, am fifteen years old when I begin this journal. We have been reading Louisa Gurney's (Grandpapa's sister's) private journal and that has given us a rage for them which I hope will last. I have, for two years kept a short diary, but that is rather dull, as one cannot write what one thinks of things unless it is private. So this is going to be *thoroughly* private, and my sisters Vi and Amy are going to keep one too. *This* is not going to be a *religious* journal like Great Aunt Louisa's but only what we do and what I think of things and people.

We six lived in London *very* happily with our darling Papa and Mama till the year 1867 when, within five weeks of each other, Papa and Mama died. I cannot write anything about this – it was *too* dreadful. We then came to live with Grandpapa Gurney at North Runcton Hall, near King's Lynn, where we have lived ever since.

I will now write a short description of my brothers and sisters and myself.

Amy, my eldest sister, is seventeen, she has fair, rather reddish hair, blue eyes, rather a large nose and a nice, but rather sneering mouth. She is rather tall, with a nice figure and we think her pretty. She is very like Papa. In her character she is *very* lively, excitable and very changeable in some things. She is easily put into a passion, but it never lasts long. She is awfully fond of *teasing*, which she does to perfection. She is very fond of dress, but I do not think she is exactly *vain*. She is clever and has a good deal of conversation. I do not think she is *altogether* quite straightforward with everybody, of course I do not mean with us, but I mean she would not have the slightest objection to do little *faussetés* to other people. She is very generous and kind (except when she is teasing). She draws very well and paints too, but she does not do either much because she so seldom has a *rage* for them. She plays the piano *beautifully* and can play anything by ear and she is *never* tired of it. She is secretly rather romantic, *I* think. Ever since she was quite little she has been having *flames* for people. She *now* says she is *never* going to marry because she has been (or has thought herself) very much in love with a certain Mr. Herbert [Ivor Herbert, afterwords Lord Treowen] who she met in London at Abbey Lodge, and who danced with her and made himself *remarqué* of her. He is now married, but she says she likes him just as much as ever (though of course she does not really), and is always talking of her 'darling Ivor', for that is the name he is blessed with. I wonder who she will be in love with next?

I, Laura, am the next one of the family. (We had a brother between Amy and I who died when he was two months old, his name was Thomas Hay.) I have brown, rather slimy, thickish hair, small brownish eyes, very far apart, a very ugly nose, a pretty mouth and a nice shaped face, only too fat. I have not the least a nice figure and am about the same height as Amy. I shall not write much about my character because I do not think one *can* know oneself very well. I am *conceited* I think, but yet I could not say what of, for I *have* nothing to be conceited of. I am rather *forward* occasionally and say stupid things, (I *used* to be much more than I am), the consequence is that I *very* often *hate* myself. I am awfully impertinent sometimes (though nothing like I used to be), it comes on in fits now and then and when it goes leaves me filled with regret. I do not *think* I am very selfish but I am rather jealous about little things and also rather *envious* about *little* things, such as *toilettes*, which I am very fond of. I think I am very affectionate by nature, although I do not show it much. I am generally kind and good-natured, but not altogether good-tempered, as I am rather often in a bad mind. I like chaffing awfully and can generally answer anybody who chaffs me. I do not think I am clever, but I have a sprinkling of useful information. I can draw very well and am *very* fond of it, but I cannot play the least. I am *awfully* fond of reading and I am *not in love*, and that is quite enough about me. I am, I forgot to put, rather lazy and do not do things as well as I could, lessons, I mean. It's such a bore, or too much trouble.

Violet, my next sister, is thirteen and nine months. She was *awfully* pretty when she was little and will be, rather, when she is grown-up, although she is not *now*. She has very dark, thick, rather frizzy hair, nice dark eyes, a dreader nose and a rather dreader mouth. ('Dreader' is a family word meaning *inferior*.) She has a white skin, but not a nice complexion, except in the evening. She has a nice figure and is awfully tall for her age, as she is the same height as Amy and I. I do not exactly know what to put about her character, she is awfully reserved and rather shy. She is very quiet, except with us. She has not the *least* vanity and would not care if she was dressed in a sack, which is rather nice, only it can be carried too far. She is not the *least* industrious and has no energy in her, she sometimes sits doing nothing, with her hands before her, till I long to shake her. She is *awfully* obstinate sometimes and very rarely gives up anything. She is neither jealous, envious nor greedy, but she is *very* dainty. We are none of us very tidy, I am afraid. Vi has one very disagreeable thing about her which is that she occasionally says such *disgustingly* true things about one, out loud and to one, without caring who is in the room. It is so tiresome because one cannot answer them because one *feels* that they are true. (She has, I am glad to say, quite left off that now.) She is very straightforward and not the *least* romantic and is *very* jolly. I think she can see people's characters very well. I wonder what she will put about me in her journal? She draws *beautifully* but cannot play much.

I shall now write about Clemence. She is not really our sister but our governess, but she is quite young and has been with us for seven years, therefore we love her, treat her and think of her as our sister. She is twenty-seven and a Belgian. She has most beautiful fair, golden hair, a very fair, pale complexion, very good eyebrows, but dreader eyes, a very good long, straight Grecian nose, not at all a good mouth, but a beautiful figure. She is not the *least* vain although she is so pretty. She is very generous, rather quick-tempered and very prejudiced about certain people and things, though for others she will always make allowances. *We* all *adore* her. She is quite like one of us and I could not exist here a moment if *she* was not with us.

Tom, my eldest brother, is twelve, but he will be thirteen next month. He is not the *least* nice looking but he has a *very* clever face. He has sandy hair, is covered with freckles and has small, dreader blue eyes, a hideous nose, which he is always blowing and sniffling with, not a bad small mouth and very white teeth, much the best of the family. His character is, I am afraid, *not very* nice – (I do not think I *ought* to have written that, but I have made a sort of *vow* not to scratch out.) He is not straightforward, is greedy and has *awfully* bad manners (in the *cercle intime!*) He is passionate at times but, on the other hand, he is not the *least* proud, is generous and affectionate and is always sorry after he has done wrong and *does sometimes* give up, which Ernest (my other brother) never does. Tom, although he is plain and Papa was good-looking, is very like him at times. I forgot to say that Tom is tiny, reaching about up to my shoulder, but we hope he will grow, as both Papa and Mama were very tall. Tom cannot draw the least, nor play, but he has a very good ear for music. He is *secretly* rather proud of us three. He is awfully amusing sometimes and makes us *roar* with laughter, but sometimes he is in what Ernest calls a 'bate'. Both the boys are at school at Twyford, near Winchester, where they have been for two years. Before that they were at a school near Lowestoft, at a Miss Ringer's, Tom was only eight and Ernest six when they went there. Tom is going to Wellington College when he leaves Twyford as he is, I believe, going into the Army, which I don't like at all as I feel he is sure to be either shot or dreadfully wounded like Papa was.

Ernest, my second brother, is eleven. He is, we think simply lovely. He has dark brown awfully thick *clots* of rather curly hair, a very white skin (now awfully tanned and freckled, as it is summer, from going in the sun with nothing but a blue and white cricket cap on the back of his head), red cheeks, blue eyes, a lovely little nose, angelic mouth, and an awfully pretty-shaped face – altogether the sort of face that one longs to kiss. He has no character hardly, he is entirely governed by Tom. He does *whatever* Tom does and has also *dreadful* manners, but I think he is more selfish, but very affectionate. The thing about those boys is that they never obey anybody except Grandpapa and he does not *know* everything about them. What they want is a father over them, for they really *do* want keeping in order dreadfully. Ernest cannot draw either but he has a sweet voice and is very clever. (I forgot to say that we can all five swim and we go to some awfully jolly swimming baths in Lynn.)

I have not written yet about my dear little sister, Helen. She is seven and a half, rather pretty, with brown hair and a very nice complexion, pretty dark eyes, but rather sunken, an ugly nose and a sweet little mouth. She is too young for me to write much about her character. She has a very good idea of drawing and plays nicely on the piano. She is very clever and sometimes very amusing. She is vain and inclined to be jealous, awfully fond of reading and very quiet. I think it is rather dull for her having no sisters of her own age. (I forgot to put that Ernest is, I believe, going into the Navy, which I do not like at all. It will be so dreadful when he is at sea on stormy nights, he is sure to be drowned. I am not at all a good soldier's daughter!)

Grandpapa, whom we live with, is our Mama's Papa. He is very old, being eighty-two, but is happily in very good health, and will I believe live for years more. He is very kind to us and we love him very much. Of course he has old-fashioned ideas and that makes him rather fussy sometimes, especially about little things with the boys. His wife died about thirty-six years ago. He has had nine children (one died when it was a baby, and one of his daughters died after she was married, about eighteen years ago).

I have written a much longer description of us all than I meant to, but it did swell out so, without my knowing it, I also think I have said too much about our looks and perhaps not been quite charitable enough in my descriptions of them, because when I read it over, it seems rather horrid to write that they are selfish and greedy and all those sort of things about people I love so awfully much as I love them all. I really have a good mind to tear this up and burn it, and yet I feel sure that if I do I shall regret it some day, so I shall let it live.

I am now going to write a short account of our present home, Runcton, and the servants. It is a very pretty house, large but not too much so. There are forty-three rooms – it was a cottage when Grandpapa first came here, about sixty years ago and he built on to it. The garden is *very* pretty, not *very* large but so nice – I like it better than any other I have ever seen. The school-room (which we have made much the prettiest room in the house) is on the same floor as our bedrooms. The boys sleep upstairs, close to the nurseries. That is enough about the house. I will now write about the servants.

Guddy (Gordon) is the housekeeper and manager of everything. She has been here for fifty years, but is quite well and always running about. She is Scottish and has been very nice-looking, she is very small and has little grey curls. She always wears a very large crinoline and little cotton capes in the house. She is very kind, but she often raves at one and tells awfully long stories so quickly that one cannot understand a *single word*.

Mrs. Quick is the cook, she has been here about twenty years and is rather nice, but she has a very bad temper. She makes very good things for late dinner but not for our dinner. The kitchen maid, Lydia, but called Ann, has been here about eight years; the housemaid, Ellen Palgrave, is very nice, she has been here fifteen years. The under-housemaid is Jane Jex, a nice, good-tempered girl, she has been here about two years and is always having the toothache. Then we have two maids, Anne and Stanbrook. Anne is the school-room maid, she is very nice indeed, has been with us two years and was our nursery maid a long time ago in London. Stanbrook is our maid and Helen's nurse, she and Anne make our dresses. I do not care for Stanbrook, she is not at all good-tempered and is so pretentious, she is always trying to order *us* about. Then there is the butler, Durnford, and Grand-papa's valet, James Case. Then there is a man whose name is

James, but he is always called John – he's the footman. The coachman is Robert Betts, a very bad-tempered man. The stable man is George Palgrave, he is very nice, his wife is the dairy woman and takes care of the hens. The dairy man is William Smith, but he is always called Taggy. The gardener is James Trower, I do not like him, he is always taking loads of his friends round the garden and giving them fruit and flowers, and then saying that we have eaten the fruit and took the flowers. There are three under-gardeners, Carr, Largin and Harris, they have all been here ages. That's all about the servants.

Grandfather has forty-six grandchildren, making for us forty first cousins on Mama's side. I should think we had hundreds and hundreds of second and third cousins, many of whom I have never seen and am not going to write about.

Childhood with our Parents

My father and mother lived when they were first married at No.
20 Eaton Square. After my arrival they moved to No. 8 Queen's
Gate, then rather new houses. There were gardens over the way
and the Horticultural Gardens lower down. This is the first home
I remember – a large conventional London house. Thanks to my
mother being by nature artistic and in many ways in advance of
her date, it had some charm of colour and arrangement. If I shut
my eyes I can still wander in that house, especially the drawing-
room, a large double room full of pink light from rose colour
walls and pink transparent curtains in the long windows. The
carpet was dark moss green and I thought it lovely – just like
fairyland. The furniture was French, with gold and white cupids
supporting tables and consoles, and long looking-glasses.

Unlike many London people, although my mother went out a
good deal, she had us very often with her. We three girls and little
Tom drove with her by turns every afternoon in the open carriage.
Generally at four o'clock we called for my father at the Horse
Guards. I can see him, on his crutches, coming carefully down the
steps of the archway leading to his office and always with a smile
and cheery greeting for us children, and such a loving look for
my mother.

I can vividly see my father, who was A.D.C. to Queen Victoria, going off with my mother to a Drawing Room [one of
Queen Victoria's Courts which were then held in the afternoons],
in his scarlet and gold uniform with the sash and aiguillettes, my
mother in white satin, her long train edged with the eyes of
peacocks' feathers and gold beads – in her hair white plumes and
veil. I thought her very lovely, as indeed she was, with her dark
hair, blue eyes and beautiful ivory pale face.

Another of my earliest recollections is of my elder sister Amy

dressed as a fairy, in a white frock with a wreath of silver wheat-
ears round her gold curls, standing up straight on my father's
outstretched hand, his elbow to his side, as he sat in his wheel-
chair in the dining-room at Queen's Gate. It was a feat of strength
that deeply impressed me. I do not think I was more than four
years old, if so much, but Papa was always to us a very wonderful
person, who, as we hung round his chair in the children's hour
after tea, would draw delightful pictures for us, make wonderful
shadows on the wall, or play and sing to the guitar gay Spanish
songs, and tell us stories to make us laugh. To be sorry for Papa
never once crossed our minds, as children. Of course he walked
on crutches, and went up and down stairs in the lift, but that was
just Papa. Only long afterwards did I understand the quiet,
patient endurance with which he bore his trial so that no shadow
of it was felt by those about him.

Once I remember a cavalry regiment rode past our house in a
thick fog – just a glint of scarlet and gold and a horse's head showing here and there. My father made us all look from the windows,
saying, 'Children, that is just what a battle is like, it is about all
you can see and the noise is terrific.' This was, of course, before
the days of smokeless powder. Another time he told us of Florence Nightingale, nursing in the hospital at Scutari. I was too
small to understand and thought it odd a nurse should have a
bird's name, and was still more confused when he said, 'She would
not nurse the officers – we used to see nice little custard puddings
carried past – but they were for the men, we only had rough
orderlies to take care of us.' I had no idea what a 'rough orderly'
could be but it sounded very dreadful.

I never remember being petted in the nursery. Perhaps there
were too many of us, but we had nice, merry, young nursery
maids who used to sing songs with us. One favourite song as I
understood it was:

> *Girls and boys, come out to play*
> *The moon doth shine as bright as day*
> *Come with a hoop or come with a ball*
> *Come with a Goodwin or not at all!*

This seemed a little depressing, for I knew well that Goodwin, our nurse, would never have taken us out to play by the light of the moon – nothing less likely! Nurse Goodwin always had a birch rod hanging over the chimney-piece in the nursery, as a sort of emblem of authority, for she was never allowed to use it and could only crash it down on to the unoffending table when we disobeyed her, which I suppose was a relief to her feelings, but it was not an endearing habit. 'I'll flay you alive!' was one of her favourite threats, so she cannot have been an ideal Nanny. These same birch rods were made expressly for us by a Park Keeper in Kensington Gardens, a grim old man who was a friend of Goodwin's. We used to call at his Lodge for these rods of office, the room always smelt of wood smoke, and even now that peculiar pungent smell and birch rods are linked together in my mind.

A horrid dark hour of my childhood in Goodwin's reign remains with me. I, with perfect innocence, asked my mother if I might have some of the jam Nurse Goodwin kept in the night nursery cupboard. Perhaps some enquiries and blame followed but of this I knew nothing, and deeply resented being attacked and told I was a wicked Tell Tale. In spite of my tears a horrid tongue of scarlet flannel was roughly tied round my neck, and the two nursery maids and the others danced in a ring about me and sang the shameful words:

Tell Tale Tit – Her tongue shall be slit
And all the dogs in the town shall have a little bit!

I covered my face with my hands and wept bitterly, for I had meant no wrong. Of course all these episodes were unknown to my mother. Goodwin's somewhat austere reign came to an abrupt end. I believe now the poor woman heard some bad news, for I see her with an open letter in her hand, falling to the ground, the maids gathered round trying to revive the poor soul. But for us, strange to say, it had but one interpretation and the tidings flew round the nursery, in horrified whispers, 'Gooey is drunk!'

But there are many happy memories to set in the balance, delightful half-holidays spent with our father and mother, in

summer at the Zoo, or Chiswick or Kew Gardens, when we
children trailed after them, picking the many wild flowers in the
deep grass, or long drives in the open carriage to Rose Gardens,
near London, bringing home great fragrant bunches, or to the
Crystal Palace where we saw Leotard, in spangles, descend a
long spiral on a ball, and even stayed for the fireworks on summer
evenings, to drive home nestled down like a bird in the depths of
the big carriage, dreaming of the showers of stars falling like
fairies from the night sky.

In winter there were indoor sights to visit; the Polytechnic,
where the scientific side passed me by entirely. The Diving Bell
seemed quite everyday, the real attraction was the stall of glass
ships, stags and other toys, spun like magic before one's eyes.
Then there were the joys of the Soho and Baker Street Bazaars,
and the rare delights of the Circus and the Christmas Pantomimes
and many children's parties, so that, compared to the years that
followed we appear to have led lives crowded with incident and
all set about with affection.

My sister Helen's arrival was a wonderful surprise. My father
sent for us children one January morning, and as we stood round
his wheel-chair he told us the great news that we had a baby
sister, just arrived. In my delight I jumped right into his arms and
hugged him close. He let us write long lists of girls' names, from
which three were chosen – Helen Cecil Margaret. Then for the
Christening we all had new blue poplin dresses with Irish lace
collars, and hats trimmed with blue velvet and wreaths of white
daisies – all three sisters alike.

I have always been fond of clothes, ever since I can remember,
so these blue frocks were a joy. In those days Amy had naturally
more privileges than I had. I felt envy, even to tears, when with
her hair beautifully *crêpé* (with hot irons, by my mother's French
maid), and wearing a little white cloak, fan and gloves, she was
taken by Mama to a mysterious amusement called 'Mellon's
Concert'. I wept at remaining at home in bed, although I did
not know what joys awaited her, and only knew a melon as a
delicious-looking and unobtainable fruit!

Every summer my parents took a house in the country for July and later they took us to the seaside, and generally to Runcton, before we came back to London for the winter – I suppose the usual routine for children of our day. In this way I remember first a summer at Northrepps Cottage, a very pretty place near Cromer, belonging to my mother's aunt, Lady Buxton. Here I had a birthday, I believe of three, perhaps four – anyhow my sister Violet and I used to go, tucked up in panniers, on a Cromer donkey down to the shore, Amy riding astride the long suffering animal, so we must have been very small. I have one other recollection of Northrepps Cottage, my father and mother, having driven to the lighthouse hills, were walking together when one of my father's crutches went into a hornets' nest and broke off short, leaving my poor father entirely helpless. With great presence of mind he kept his crutch firmly in the hole, while my mother ran for the carriage and sent off in haste for another pair of crutches. Meanwhile my father sat on the ground, hearing the angry buzzing within the nest, and prepared to fight with any stray hornets, should they return and find him in possession.

One summer we had a dear old house at Hampstead, from where my father could drive down to the Horse Guards while we revelled in what was then more or less open country, for I remember picnics in leafy woods, full of wild flowers, honeysuckle and blue speedwell. The house had a square hall where on wet days we played at concerts, or perhaps 'Christy Minstrels' would be more accurate, sitting in a row singing nigger songs, beating time upon our battledores that did duty for banjos. Then what pleasure it was when our cook, an amiable creature called Mrs. Capon, very fond of us children, would give us a great lump of dough. With this pale, sickly stuff did we fashion bracelets and earrings, set with acorns and flower heads. After we wearied of this amusement the remnants of dough would be collected, rolled flat with a pencil, on the lid of a toy box, and – horrid thought – served up as a tart, the interior of currants filched from the kitchen garden, or hard green gooseberries, the crust a little grey, but what then? I can recall the voice of exquisite politeness with which this delicacy would be offered at the ensuing feasts. 'Will you have a little fruit tart?' 'Yes, please,' with a smile full of grown-up suavity and guile, 'but not any crust, please, my doctor does not allow me to eat any pastry', and so on round the party, with many suppressed giggles, was the disgusting stuff rejected by all.

Dressing up was always a joy to the family. One afternoon my father and mother, driving back late in the open carriage from London, saw a crowd of people collected outside our house, where some leads that formed a sort of balcony to our school-room could be seen from the Heath. Here, as they drove up, they saw some fantastic little figures dancing to pipe and tambourine, whirling, stamping and singing – much to the amusement of the onlookers. The tambourine was to have been handed round presently for pence, as we had seen done by seaside musicians, but the revel came to an abrupt end, and future efforts in that direction were forbidden.

In one of my mother's journals she says of my brother Tom, aged four, 'He is backward with his sums, but gets on nicely with his French.' My brother Ernest taught himself to read at three years old. I weighed heavily on the other side of the balance, having through some fever lost the rudiments of the three Rs, most painfully acquired, and I had the mortification of learning to read for the second time at the mature age of six. I was what might be called a late flowerer, and the music lessons that Amy sailed through with such flying colours were to me great tribula-tion. Even now I resent the hours spent in hopeless effort to acquire some futile tune on the piano, but it was the custom for girls to learn to play, so I cannot justly blame my parents for expecting me to take my share in the dismal chorus.

The first of the instructors of our youth I can remember was an elderly female, a Miss Paget. She was a 'daily', appearing at ten o'clock and suffering a total eclipse at twelve; two long hours at which to quaff at the fount of knowledge. She seems to me to have been a large woman, and kindly, upholstered in black shiny silk, with a sleek head like a seal. I did not dislike her, but simply preferred to be idle. I had seen my father, in the mornings, looking at a mysterious object that hung on the wall in our dining-room and, after tapping it two or three times with his hand, saying, 'Ah, it will be fine today', or 'Rain again', as the case might be, and such weather always followed. In my colossal ignorance I thought our weather glass ruled the elements. Miss Paget, having once failed to come in a pea soup fog, I valiantly climbed on a chair at an opportune moment when the dining room was empty, and found that by vigorous tapping and knocking I could turn the hand round to 'Stormy', or even 'Very Stormy'. It was a nasty jar when the sun continued to shine in the sky and Miss Paget appeared as usual. In fact, after some days of these disappointments I confided to my mother my failure to work the charm as Papa did, and was promptly forbidden to touch the magic glass which, not unnaturally, had seemed to be rather out of order, from its erratic movements.

Miss Paget had a very delicate mind, or was it rather indelicate? At all events one of the questions in the *Child's Guide to Knowledge*, her great educational standby, stood thus, *What is rennet?* Who could wish to know anything so obscure, except possibly a cook much given to the making of junkets? We had no curiosity on that subject and this was as well, because the answer, which had to be learnt by heart, was shrouded in deep mystery. It contained the offending word 'stomach', and Miss Paget in her wisdom had scored it through heavily with ink. So the answer read thus, *Rennet is a preparation made from a calf's . . . ahem!* Thus were we protected against the indelicacies of life.

Dear Miss Paget, my last recollection of her is more heroic. She was in charge of us once on a visit to Grandpapa at Runcton, our parents being away. We all went to tea with the Gurney cousins at Valleyfield. In their garden was a long pond, full of weeds and water-lilies and much mud, a sloping bank led to it. Mortimer Gurney, a big boy compared to me, amused himself by running after me, threatening to throw me into the pond, no doubt for a joke, to enjoy my screams of terror. He caught me up in his arms and ran quickly down the slope, too fast to stop, and with a great splash we both fell in and disappeared below the murky water. Mortimer's conduct was not chivalrous. for he swam across the pond and scrambled out the other side, leaving me to my fate as I sank in the mud. Now was Miss Paget's chance – all false delicacy over the rennet question was forgotten and forgiven as, in her best black silk, she waded waist deep into the pond, dragged me out and up the steep bank, the other children crowding round us. I remember well the horrid feeling of the streams of muddy water in my eyes and hair, as I stood, a poor dripping little figure, saying over and over again, 'Oh, am I drowned, am I drowned?', and then the tears as with the water squelching in my shoes, and my white frock spoilt, I was led into the house – as it were in disgrace – from the merry party and the lovely afternoon, to be undressed and put to bed (always a hated punishment with us).

Miss Paget seems to disappear after that episode. She was followed by some rather nebulous figures, who reigned briefly. One I remember, a Miss Macey, red-haired and angular, also took us to Runcton, where I have a queer little picture of her in my mind wearing a white cambric dress all sprinkled over with tiny brown and yellow butterflies, made with a little cape with a frill round it, and wide brimmed hat. I thought it very attractive. In the lane, by the Park gates, rode Charles Wright, the good-looking son of Grandpapa's steward, and I suppose it was a farewell I witnessed – it could hardly have been an introduction – for, stooping from his horse as Miss Macey stood beside him, he deftly lifted her up off the ground like a doll and kissed her, replacing her carefully, greatly to the surprise of my infant mind. I do not remember any instruction filtering through from Miss Macey, so perhaps she was a holiday governess.

The first serious governess we had was called by the romantic name of Florine Prudhomme, and was to us very fascinating and new. She was French and wore plaid frocks, her hair was dark, her eyes very bright and starry, and her face cream colour. Amy was her favourite in all things and at all times, but the school-room became in her reign a very interesting place. She was young and had, I fancy, what is called personal magnetism, for we all adored her. She played and sang charmingly to us and even tried to teach me some of her songs, from *Kathleen Mavourneen* to *Villikins and his Dinah*. I think she was with us a year, perhaps two, but gradually she became very secretive, whispering with Amy of mysterious people by their initials. This was very galling to me as number two, and out in the cold, so I took refuge with Vi and our dolls. I now know that Miss Prudhomme had become a Roman Catholic and when she left us it was to be a nun in a London Convent. My parents were sorry as they liked her. We children gave her a silver watch and chain as a parting present, for the nuns were not allowed to wear gold. We were sad when she left and all went to visit her in the Convent, hardly recognizing our pretty Florine in her close cap and black habit as a novice.

Anyhow we wept when she departed, and I can see us three, sitting on her trunk, crying and making our moan over the new governess my mother had engaged. 'Oh, Mama, I am sure she will be ugly and unkind! Oh, Mama, does she wear spectacles? Oh, Mama, I am sure we shall hate her!' My mother smiled and comforted us, telling us the lady from Brussels who was coming was quite young and pretty and we should all be very fond of her. Her name was Clemence Vleminck. Fond of her? Well, indeed, she was right, and Heaven must have guided her choice. Mademoiselle Vleminck's father had lost his fortune, so she and her sister Marie came to teach in London. Her first place was with us and my mother the first English lady she had seen. She played a large part in all the years of our childhood, and I know influenced us for good in many ways. As she had not herself had time for more advanced education (she was only nineteen) she could not make it interesting to our eyes. She was with us for a year before we lost our father and mother, to whom she was devoted. The fact that she had known them and been part of our home life was the great link between us when after the débacle of our world, we went to live at Runcton.

The end of our happy childhood came all too soon. In 1867 my mother had arranged to go over to Paris for a week, with the de Bunsen cousins, my father to rooms in Park Street for a short time, and we children with governess and nurses to Runcton, where they would join us later. I still remember the blank feeling of disappointment as we children came down to prayers, the morning I thought they would come to us, and Grandpapa said, 'I am sorry, children, but dear Papa and Mama cannot come today for Mama is not well,' and he sighed. That was the beginning of the end of our happy childhood – I know now that my mother took a chill, as they thought, on the journey from Paris, where she had been radiantly well and happy. In a few days she was worse, the doctor said it was typhoid fever, caught in Paris.

Only the dim echoes of all the anxiety reached us children. We knew nothing of the agony of my poor father, ever at her side, in the fight to save her precious life. He broke down in health and could not sleep, so that when the doctor thought the crisis was past he persuaded him to join us children in the country. But he looked so pale and sad we almost feared him. He came for a Sunday, but the next day was telegraphed for to London as Mama was worse. He was there when she died – aged only thirty-six – and to my father it gave his death wound.* He only survived her five weeks, he had no wish to live on without her, and we children were too young to bring him comfort. Once only do I remember sitting near my father, stroking his hand and trying, in my small way, to convey the sympathy I felt.

A cousin of his, Mrs. Ware Scott, who was devoted to him, came to see him the evening before he died. She said, 'St. Vincent, you are looking much better tonight.' He smiled at her, shook his head, and said quietly, 'Oh, no, I shall not live through the night.' And so it was.

The news of my father's death came to me in a strange way. My sister Vi and I shared the night nursery, and when our maid called us that October 2nd we eagerly asked how Papa was. 'Better', she said, with a curious grave look, but we must be very

---

* Eight years later, Laura at the age of seventeen described in her journal how the news of her mother's death had reached the children, who had been sent from their grandfather's house to stay at Yarmouth with their governess.

good and quiet. So like mice we dressed and crept down, past his door to our school-room breakfast, only to find our governess and Amy both in tears. (Tom, Ernest and Helen were away at Grandmama Troubridge's). Afterwards we three sisters were sent for to the library, where we found my poor old grandmother had arrived, as usual in her heavy crêpe dress, her face like an ivory image of grief. My father was the last of her four sons. There, too, was Aunt Chatty, weeping hysterically, rocking to and fro. They embraced us as we stood silent and shy before their tears. 'You poor, poor children', they said and kissed us, trembling with emotion. It was very puzzling to me, and, to silence a fearful doubt that rose chill at my heart, I asked in a frightened whisper, 'Grandmama, are we orphans?' She, poor soul, broke down at that, and as she sobbed she told us the sorrowful truth that our father had gone from us too.

Then, after we had all wept for a while, the great and vital question, strangely enough, was put to us children by my grand-mother, 'Would you rather live with us at Queen's Gardens, or with your Grandfather Gurney at Runcton, tell us truly?' With one voice we answered, 'At Runcton with Grandpapa, please.' And so it was settled. Was this another blow to those sorrowing women, or a relief? I have often wondered, but this was how our fate at the moment was decided.

Childhood with Grandpapa

Runcton was the best, indeed the only home for us. With the odd inconsequence of childhood, the thought that we were leaving No. 8 Queen's Gate for ever never once crossed my mind. A visit to Runcton had always been considered next to Paradise itself, so almost eagerly we left the old home for the new. Grandpapa came himself to fetch us, that very day, with James, his valet. Grandpapa was already an old man, with snow white hair, very thin and upright. He had lived alone for many years, but seemed pleased at the coming of us six 'young things', as he called us.

I still remember that evening as we travelled down to Lynn through the darkness, that alone a great event in our lives. I have a picture of it in my mind of the carriage blinds all drawn down, Grandpapa so grave and silent in one corner, we three in our black frocks, and our governess, keeping close together that chill October evening. At nine, long past our bedtime, we arrived at Lynn where a message was given that we children were to sleep that night at the Globe Inn. An odd plan, the why and wherefore I do not know, but we drove to this large old-fashioned Inn, in the Market Place, and at last found rest after the long, strange day, Vi and I sleeping hand in hand in a huge four-poster, Amy in a little bed beside us. Many kind and sympathetic maid servants came in to have a look at 'the poor Children' as we were often to be called in those days.

The next day the Runcton omnibus, afterwards irreverently called 'the bathing machine' (which it strangely resembled), came to fetch us. I remember that first drive up the Approach, and the strange feeling that we were not singing and laughing, as we always did on those occasions. Uncle Sommy [Gurney – known as Uncle Tum], in a black knickerbocker suit and Norfolk jacket, very tall and handsome, was at the gate to meet us. He jumped on the step of the carriage as we drove up to the house and gave us a delightful welcome. Dear Uncle Sommy, he was very good to us in those early days; in spite of his six children at Valleyfield I think we saw him every day. He was always ready to care for us and all our interests. In the happy old days Grandpapa used to be in the porch to greet us, laughing and saying, 'Capitalibus! Capitalibus! Here we are – here we are – now I must have a kiss from each.' But that day all was sombre and quiet, there was no merry greeting for us as we came to our new home.

A few days after our arrival at Runcton, Uncle Sommy sent for us early one morning and told us he was going to London, to No. 8 Queen's Gate, and, strange tidings, that we might each choose a present from home. We never thought he meant we might have any of the real grown-up things that belonged to Papa and Mama, and this was not explained to us. So, sad to say, we each asked for some silly object of our childish admiration. Amy was more ambitious and asked for a case of gay, foreign stuffed birds, about which Papa used to tell her stories. I asked for a wax gypsy figure with a tray of tiny toys to sell, that lived under a glass case – I thought it rather like a doll, and Vi set her heart on three little wax babies on three gilt chairs, also under a tiny glass case, that she used to be allowed to play with in my mother's room. It was sad to have missed the chance of a real souvenir from our home where there were so many artistic and interesting things we might have chosen had we understood.

Years after we so regretted that all the family things had been sold – books, china, sketches, my father's swords, the field-glasses with which he saw the enemy coming up in the misty morning (and so prevented a surprise attack on his Battery at Inkerman), and a pistol that was shot in two at his side at the Alma. Such things as these, of no real intrinsic value, but intensely interesting to us as we grew up, were all swept away by the carelessness, or want of thought, of relations who only wished the sad business over and done with, and so ordered everything to be sold indiscriminately.

Our nice old housemaid, Harriet Thirkel, all honour to her, was so distressed to see the photographs and all the personal treasures go, that before the men came to mark the lots for the sale she went herself to the drawing-room and rescued all she could for us, filling her apron full, our story books too. They came in a big box to Runcton, I can remember unpacking it and the strange feeling that those things were ours now.

Amy's treasure cabinet was sent down – but not mine. I had asked Uncle Sommy to bring me something from home that was my very own, it was a tiny white china cup and saucer, with coral red feet and handles, probably worth a shilling or two, but to me of rare beauty. I loved it and when I had tea with my mother I always used this little cup and saucer, it was kept in the drawing-room. But it could not be found, so Uncle Sommy in his kindness brought me instead a fine white cup of Oriental china, rare and valuable, but alas I received it with tears. Where indeed were the lovely coral feet and handles? This was not my darling cup and saucer, this ugly old thing! Indignantly, when he left, I put it on the stairs – I would have none of it, and left it to its fate, which was quickly decided by Grandpapa's valet James, who coming downstairs promptly stamped on it. It was smashed and the fragments thrown into the dustbin, but only for a time. A letter followed quickly from Grandmama Troubridge – where, oh where, was a Chinese cup of rare old porcelain she had brought over to show my father, nowhere could it be found? The dustbin was searched and, skilfully mended, the poor ill-used cup was returned to Grandmama with many apologies for the accident.

The garden at Runcton was like a group of gardens. We had our favourite haunts – though all were free to us. First there were 'our gardens', to which we had succeeded the original owners – our uncles and aunts, having no further use for those queer little box-edged plots, with the green painted summer house, full of small garden tools, that stood at one end. The other special playground was the old bowling green, where a swing had been put up in the branches of a big oak tree at one corner, and a croquet set provided. 'The Museum,' as we called a little house, an old cottage I suppose in that garden, was where our pets were housed. Then we loved the Long Walk, where the first snowdrops grew and, later, the purple rhododendrons. There was the Round Pond, where the old tench came up to breathe and the moorhens built their careless nests in the rushes. The North Walk, where the Name Tree stood – carved over with many family initials. The 'Family Coach', a big old garden seat, grand for various games, stood under some huge elms, the remains of an avenue that wandered across the Park. Then there was the Pinetum, rather an unpopular place with us, not lending itself to many games, and the Vinery garden, where the grapes and strawberries were kept carefully locked up by the head gardener, no friend to us, but where the wall could at places be climbed with the help of some old espalier pears, when James Trower, our enemy, was known to be awa' at his dinner. And now I have not told of the South Walk, that bordered like a bright ribbon, the old grey wall, festooned with roses and wisteria and sweetest starry jasmine. It was a blaze of bright colour all the summer through – spangled over with butterflies and humming bees – and there, in winter, violets and Christmas roses could be found.

Indoors there was the library, a long, low double room, with hundreds of books and the peculiar atmosphere they create – a big oak fireplace at either end – and many large tables groaning with heavy volumes. The drawing-room had a quiet faded dignity of its own. The big armchairs and sofas chintz-covered, with bunches of lilac on a white ground and the curtains the same – old oriental china in cabinets, and great jars of potpourri. But over all was a stillness of a long ago past, helped perhaps by the large red velvet-covered table, spread with white and gold gift books, that formed an island in the centre of the room, this and the absence of any flowers, or signs of occupation, the grand piano closed, a harp silent in its case, gave the feeling of a room long asleep, where any modern touch would have been out of place – for it had been just so since my grandmother lived in the thirties.

The school-room wing was our kingdom – on the first floor and shut off by a swing-door – as were also my Grandfather's rooms. The school-room looked straight down the Approach. This would have been a greater advantage if more people had used the drive! However there was always the possibility of something coming, so it was worth looking out, especially during lesson time! The long school-room passage was papered by my uncles long ago with pictures, many very amusing. It led to our rooms. Vi and I shared a room, with a beautiful old carved fireplace. The nursery itself, was a long narrow, double room, shaped for games, with a curtain across for acting and a dear old dolls' house like a country mansion, at one end, in a sort of alcove, the nursery cupboards, where the lavender blue tea-set lurked, at the other end. Windows here and there, with window seats and big cupboards for toys. There were six doors to this room and outside on the nursery landing was a place of mystery, a sort of lumber room, called 'The Glory Hole', but out of bounds for us. Our school-room cupboard, outside that little kingdom of ours, contained the china tea-set, buff lined with white. Close by, down two steps, with double doors, was the Den, our own little play-room, serving in turns as a comfortable villa for an amazing number of dolls. Sometimes it was arranged as an attractive little kitchen, hung round with small pots and pans and everything the heart of a cook could desire – except, by the way, any kind of kitchen range or oven!

Clemence Vleminck, our last governess, being all that was left to us of the old life, we clung to her and lavished on her deep affection, which she repaid with love and unfailing sympathy. She was tall and slight, and we called her Clem. She wore her hair in a pale gold chignon, or bun, like a silk cocoon. I can see it now and often watched it when I ought to have been learning my lessons.

Clem had a high standard of truth and honesty, worth much erudite instruction to us. '*La vérité avant tout*' was one of her maxims, and '*surtout rien de faux*'. In later years when we rebelled against some tiresome order of Grandpapa's, she would stop all discussion, saying, '*Enfin votre Grandpère l'a dit et cela doit être*'.

Fine of her when it would have been so easy to win popularity by evading his often harsh rules.

I think she was frankly as bored with our lessons as we were. She taught entirely from the book, which I had a horrid feeling I could have done myself. French she did impart, we can all talk fluently, and very useful it is. As for the rest, the methods and books then in use were much to blame. French spelling and grammar were the terrors of my youth. A few words of explanation in rapid French that were enough for Amy, two years older and very quick, left me hopelessly fogged. A lesson I dreaded was *dictée*, too fast for me so that I hurried on with whole sentences jumbled up, and afterwards the order, *soulignez les participes, s'il vous plaît*. Oh why had I never the courage to own I had no idea what they were? I saw Amy, with an unfurrowed brow, neatly underlining a word here and there, yes – all very well – but which words? Disgrace inevitably followed this lesson, when in despair after much puzzled thought I would count eight words and underline the ninth. Eight words again, and then another word, just as it happened, would be *souligné*. No wonder disaster followed.

I must confess I disliked one and all of my lessons. Yes, not even drawing was exempt from the ban in my mind, only perhaps poetry in which I felt a charm and could learn well and quickly by heart. Indeed this useful talent was the salvation of my schoolroom days, for we had to learn all our lessons verbatim, and here I was far beyond the brilliant Amy, so intimate with *participes*. She had to weave in a story, or odd sentence to give her the clue to those long lists of towns with their exports, imports and population that we so detested and called by the name of 'Jography'.

Dear Clem's efforts were supplemented by several masters. On Mondays came the music master from Lynn. In my journals kept from the age of fifteen, this day always figured as Black Monday. Reddie was the name of the man who taught us, or pretended to. He was the organist of St. Margaret's Church in Lynn, the son of the man who, in his day, had trudged over to Runcton to teach music to our mother and aunts; these were his claims to fame. His claims to infamy were many in our eyes. I suppose he was a good-natured man, but no musician, and quite unfitted for the post. He was fat, scented, greasy and garrulous, with flowing curls and red cheeks. We really loathed him as he grunted beside us. One of his precepts, as he swept backwards and forwards on the piano in untidy arpeggios used to be, 'never mind the notes, so long as you get the noise', and for this instruction Reddie was paid. If Vi and I played a duet he would beat time, with bent knuckles, on our shoulders in a peculiarly aggravating way, getting harder and harder as the strains of *Qui vive?* or *Zampa* became faster and faster. Amy, lucky one, was quickly and mercifully emancipated from his thrall. She had good lessons from a German, Herr Ludwig, who came once a week from London, and was a musician.

I dare say I never could have played, my heart and mind being given up to drawing, but Vi considers Reddie and his evil teaching responsible for her musical talent being snuffed out at an early age. Once, after many grunts and groans he delivered himself of this opinion, 'See 'ere, young lady, I'll give ye a piece of advice, never 'ave yer mother-in-law in yer 'ouse', which opens up a field of speculation but not allied in any way to the science of harmony.

At twelve o'clock, three times a week, came the village schoolmaster, Mr. William Orton, called by us 'Mistroughton', his department being arithmetic and geography. He was a kind but weary looking man, with a flowing Abraham-like beard, a long upper lip and a bald head. He had an odd pompous manner, but we liked him and marvelled at his complete knowledge of arithmetic in all its hateful roots and branches. He never referred to a book, the multiplication table, dodged any way, was a refreshing breath to his nostrils. Dear Mr. Orton, he once gave forth the opinion that, 'Miss Lorra was the gem', but it cannot have been founded on my intelligence at arithmetic. In geography time he had a habit of drawing invisible maps with his long nailed forefinger on the green woolly school-room tablecloth. We were supposed to say which country he portrayed, but the fact was that scraping the cloth set our teeth violently on edge and distracted our attention so that, unless it was Italy, always drawn as an unmistakable human leg, with a large bulging calf, the trick was really impossible to guess. But he never bothered and the *séance* ended at one, with certain stereotyped remarks to Clem on the beauty of the weather, or the 'foliage', or some allusion to Shakespeare whom he always called 'the Bard of Avon'.

Tuesday afternoons we had our drawing master from Lynn. First old Mr. Ladbrook, a very ancient man who observed our ambitious efforts with much wheezy amusement, and would correct them with a soft pencil held in a purple tremulous hand. I think time or death removed old 'Laddy', as then for a while we had a very clever master who came over from Norwich. He brought us casts to draw from and taught us certain technical things, such as how to make a clear and accurate outline. He had a curious name, Claude Lorraine Richard Wilson Nursey, so I suppose he came of artistic stock. But unfortunately he also died.

After his era for many dull years we had lessons from Mr. Baines. A silent, reserved man was poor old Bainey. He always wore a snuff-coloured overcoat and a round, flat sealskin cap, summer or winter, poised over his long, pointed nose, grey wisps of hair showing all round. If we drove past him on the Lynn road he never looked up, but seemed to know by some occult power who passed, and gently lifted his cap and replaced it with a perfectly wooden stare ahead. He taught us water colour sketching after the matter of Aaron Penley, whose methods he faithfully followed. Whatever the subject, you worked it up slowly in three defined stages of colour, no dashing short cuts allowed. We worked entirely from flat copies, mostly mountains in Wales. How I loathed them from my heart. Only two hours this weekly lesson lasted, and yet how slowly the minutes passed. Curious to remember, and the *ennui* of it all, but thanks to Bainey's lessons we had some nice drawing materials, and every spare minute of my time I spent in drawing, as we all did, for pleasure. But never mountains in Wales, always figures, fancies, fairies and the like. Bainey's was a very gentle rule, when we asked his advice he usually murmured, 'Well, that's optional, dear', which did not help much, or he would say, 'It might be a more agreeable tint, Miss', but that was very definite for him. It was unlucky that when we asked him for figure subjects we were only given highly stippled groups of orange- or apple-sellers, wrapped in bunchy plaid shawls, with no features to speak of, under dusky archways. Amy, later on, was allowed to study oil painting with Mr. Baines because she was the eldest – not because of any special gift that way. I acquired a sort of second-hand knowledge of the art by listening to what he told her, whilst pretending to do my own work. Painting in oils was really his *métier*, and he was a clever copyist.

As for our spiritual instruction, once a week – Thursdays at eleven o'clock for twenty minutes we had a Bible lesson with Uncle Willie [the Rev. William Hay Gurney] our clergyman. I know he was both good and kind, but somehow we were not in touch with his teaching. We all sat round the school-room table and read a chapter, verse about, and then he explained it to us, but unfortunately during that time we were always anxiously saying over to ourselves the three verses we had to repeat to him at the end of the lesson. If only it had occurred to my uncle to make us repeat these verses first we might have profited more by his instructions, which I own I never remotely connected with help or guidance in our lives.

Our German master, one Herr Göebells, also came under the ban of my displeasure. Although he had lived nineteen years in England he could not speak English, and yet he expected us to learn his language in a mere three months. Thus firmly, yet fairly, did I put the case. He used to bicycle over from Lynn, smelling strongly of stale tobacco, and for an hour address us volubly: '*Verstehen ʒie?*' he would ask occasionally, to which came ever the melancholy answer, '*Nein, mein Herr.*' We did not really learn much with him.

A Miss Marsh, a second governess for Italian and literature, was added later to our school-room. I do regret not having tried to learn more with her, but a demon of idleness and inattention seemed to preside at her lessons and we foolishly rejoiced if, by drawing a red herring skilfully across the track of learning, we beguiled her to tell us of her love affairs and those of her former pupils instead of sticking to the Italian irregular verbs. Alas, only a smattering of Italian remains.

Dancing lessons always found favour in our eyes. The first I can remember were at No. 1 Queen's Gate, at Lady Aberdare's, where the younger Bruce girls were our friends. Physical culture was then represented by waving wands over one's head, or elastic straps with handles, with the toe pointed in the first position. The dancing, too, was a bit stately; *chassée croisée*, reverse, set to partners, *cavalier seul*, and back to places, and so on through the quadrilles, counting our steps the while. A slow valse and bobbing polka were rather more dashing performances. In Runcton days a class for ourselves and the cousins was held by a Mrs. Waters at the Temperance Hotel in Lynn, and when we recovered from the slightly sick feeling after driving in *en masse* in the stuffy, rumbling Runcton omnibus, it was quite amusing. Mrs. Waters was an ample lady, but very buoyant. She held her skirts well out, revealing trousers trimmed with crochet lace, white stockings and neat elastic-sided boots called, I believe, 'prunellas'.

Had we any lectures, or finishing classes? Alas no, but fortunately once free of the trammels of the school-room and its hated hours of lessons we soon realised how much, how very much, there was to learn, and Grandpapa's library (a very good one both for history and archaeology) helped us on our way. And then, too, Aunt Bache [Catherine Rachel Jones, *née* Gurney, wife of the Rev. Herbert Jones] who was really clever and cultivated, used to talk of interesting things and tell us what to read. So in time, in one way and another, more knowledge was garnered in our brains than may appear from this plain, unvarnished tale of our so-called 'education'.

Chapter 5

Grandmama Troubridge and Aunt Chatty

We three sisters, with an old family servant to take care of us, once paid a visit to Grandmama and Aunt Chatty when I was about eleven. They then lived in a dark, gloomy house in Queen's Gardens, Bayswater, full of vast, solid furniture and stores of belongings, all wreckage from larger houses and so out of proportion to their present quarters, and crowded together with mysterious boxes and pictures piled high in every dusty corner, a sort of drabbish yellow pervading the whole house. Two cousins lived with Grandmama, besides Aunt Chatty. They were Victoria and Florence Cochrane. As a household they were not gloomy, and distinctly kind to us, but somehow there was a great gulf fixed.

Grandmama had been gay and happy in her youthful days, and went into society. There is a pretty miniature of her in early married life, with bright auburn hair and smiling face, wearing a pink satin ball gown, her hair dressed high in curls, with a little openwork pearl cap and wreath of pink roses on top. I wish I had known her thus. From my earliest recollections she appears as a pyramid of black crêpe, of which her bonnet was the apex, from which hung a long, heavy black veil, generally concealing her face. In the house, without these depressing trappings, the delicate features still showed, white like ivory beneath her widow's cap. She was thin and slight and appeared to float about the room rather than walk. I see her most clearly sitting at a small round table covered with a green cloth, an open Bible and large Commentary before her, also a tray of tracts (suitable – or not – for all occasions), and still further supported by an agate box containing cough lozenges. The whole effect was very like Whistler's portrait of his mother – it recalls Grandmama vividly to my mind. But Grandmama and Aunty Chatty must speak for themselves.

For this visit we arrived fresh from our country life at Runcton, escorted by a quaint character, old Mrs. Finch, called Fighty for short. My sister Vi and I brought with us the two best and most cherished of our large doll family. When Grandmama beheld them, all dressed in their best for the journey, and clasped in our loving arms, she covered her face with her hands, saying loudly, 'Shocking – shocking, you are both too old for dollies!' So was a rift in our relations established forthwith, not that we cared for what Grandmama thought but, owing to this eccentricity of hers (as we considered it) the dolls lived a retired life in our bedrooms.

It was a curious visit. I do not remember any kind of amusement provided for us, but we liked walking with Fighty in Kensington Gardens and, better still, looking at the shop windows in Oxford Street. Most afternoons we were taken, by growler, to see various elderly relations and friends, or rather to be seen by them. As we were never told who they were or anything about them this entertainment left us cold. No presents either came our way, which might have warmed our young hearts. No, we were only peered at, till we felt like specimens in a museum, labelled 'These are poor St. Vincent's children', for so we were described.

Grandmama took us, I remember, one day to see old Lady Napier and Ettrick. I know now she was a first cousin of Grandmama's and the bosom friend of her youth. But we beheld only another black figure of untold age, lying on a sofa in a darkened room. Grandmama advanced towards her, we three children shyly following. The old lady on the sofa rose up (she seemed very tall and was also heavily draped in crêpe), stretched out her arms, saying 'Oh, Anna Maria!' 'Oh, Eliza', murmured poor Grandmama, and they continued to advance, like automatons, until they met and clasped each other in a long embrace. I regret to say we were highly amused at this, not seeing the pathos of their meeting after many sorrows, to us it appeared simply funny – especially that Grandmama should be called Anna Maria, as we had never heard her name. Very often did we naughty children enact this little scene, prancing towards each other with the greetings, followed by a wild, whirling embrace.

Family prayers were a great institution in those days.

35

Grandmama, who must have clean forgot the days of her youth, some ten minutes before the hour used to say to us in her most solemn tone, with her soft Scotch accent, 'Amy, Laura, Violet, sit on the sofa and compose your minds before family worship.' Then, after a while in filed the servants to sit in a decorous row at the far end of the dining-room. Of their household I only remember the lady's maid, Mrs. Hamerston, a weird old creature with a face like red putty and a very 'umble manner (who in a later era was found to be a secret drunkard, and rolled out of bed in the night) but then she was a shining light in the house, and the butler, Barlow, who was an avowed atheist, of the most forbidding appearance with a bald skull-like head and grim, square jaw. He also was roped in for Family Prayers (I suppose on the off chance of a word in season being heard), but he sat rigid, with a terrible expression as of one who, like the deaf adder, stopped his ears. We noticed how often Barlow seemed to hear a distant bell and scramble noisily from the room, slamming the door after him. I now think it possible some trusty pal of his was hired to ring the area bell at this hour, for prayers were very long.

Grandmama read her chosen chapter, address and prayers with solemn unction. Presently one of those tiresome maids would give a pecking cough, promptly echoed by another. Grandmama would stop reading and, fixing poor me with a mild eye, say, 'Laura, hand the lozenges to Mrs. Hamerston', and I had reluctantly to obey, take the horrid little box of peppermints, offer it to the offender and return to my place, to be received with pinches and suppressed giggles from my sisters. Then old Fighty, not to be outdone, would develop a chest cough. 'Ahem, ahem', Grandmama again, mild but firm, would stop and repeat, 'Laura, hand the lozenges to Mrs. Finch.' Why it was always my turn I do not know, but off I had to go on this oppressive service of first aid to the husky. Barlow banging from the room was a pleasing incident by comparison.

After prayers came the reward of breakfast, with nice Scotch scones, baps and the like, but then, oh then, did our hearts sink. The butler cleared the table, and relaid it as it were with large

Bibles and Commentaries, huge brown volumes. We three had to listen while Grandmama read at length from the Old Testament and then the old Commentaries to expound all that could be set forth to puzzle the youthful mind, while the clock ticked on and a wintry sun called from without. Time crept along with dragging feet for us until, at long last, a most welcome knock at the door proclaimed our deliverance was at hand, for faithful old Fighty stood without, saying apologetically, 'My Lady, I must have the young ladies now, if you please, it is past eleven o'clock. I brought them here with rosy cheeks, My Lady, and I must take them back to their Grandpapa with the same.' Good old soul, how we blessed her, hardly enduring to wait till Grandmama answered slowly, with resignation, 'Very well, Mrs. Finch, I suppose they must go.' With one whirl we were all out of the door and, dragging old Fighty with us, dancing down the long passage leading to the back library that was our bedroom, more full of lumber than most, there quickly to wrap up and fly forth into the blessed air, leaving poor old Grandmama in undisturbed enjoyment of the Commentaries.

This took place every morning, so we really needed Fighty to protect us. She was a quaint survival of older Runcton days, having been lady's maid to our mother and aunts. She adored them and often talked of their charm and kindness. One of her favourite stories was of how greatly my mother and Aunt Margaret [later Orde] had been admired when they were presented to Queen Victoria. Fighty always spoke as if she, too, had been at the Drawing Room, and described how the Queen herself turned to look at them, saying to their aunt [Lady Isabella Wemyss, née Hay] who was in Waiting, 'Two beautiful gurls, Lady Isabella.'

I wish I could convey her funny voice and manner. Poor old thing, she suffered from visions of lost grandeur, and often darkly hinted at some nebulous claims to fortune, saying if everyone had their rights she and her sister would be driving in their carriage, for Finches in Kent were the equal of the mightiest in the land. The sister, who was to have driven in this fairy coach with her, was the heroine of all poor Fighty's memoirs. She had an unbounded admiration for this dauntless person who, it appears, had had the misfortune to sit down on a needle in early youth. There being no X-rays in those far off days to help her, the needle seems to have played havoc with her young life – wandering at will about her anatomy for many years. 'Me poor sister would be out walking, taking a pleasant stroll with 'er Pa – suddenly she would cry, "Oh, the needle", and grasping 'er side (or maybe her leg) there she 'ad to stay till a chaise was fetched to take 'er home.' Even in church it did not leave her in peace, but groaning aloud, 'Oh, the needle', she had to fly in haste from her devotions. So it went on for years until, at long last, she one day cried out more loudly than ever, 'Oh, oh, the needle!' and there it was, sticking out of her elbow. She pulled it out forthwith, and, Fighty added impressively, 'the needle was as black as ink.'

We entirely believed this strange and painful history, but all the same it was fun to act the various episodes ourselves, with a very active and entirely imaginary needle. The sister who so toughly resisted these attacks died ultimately from some other complaint. Fighty used to assure us with pride, 'She went down to 'er grave with a beautiful set of teeth in her 'ead, all 'er own.' Not having ourselves arrived at the false teeth era we were not so impressed as we might have been, indeed it seemed quite natural, and we preferred the recollections of her more youthful days when her black ringlets were so magnificent that passers-by would stop the infant Finch and ask, 'Who gave you them beautiful curls?', surely rather a drivelling question, but little Fighty, undefeated, would answer pat, 'Dod A'mighty!'

A very loyal person was our poor old Finch. Nothing pleased her more when we walked with her than the sight of Queen Alexandra, then Princess of Wales, driving through the Park. Fighty would leave us in any crowd and, rushing forward, hang over the Park railings, waving her handkerchief and murmuring, 'Pretty creechur – pretty creechur', till the carriage was out of sight, when wiping tears of emotion from her eyes she returned to her charges.

Of the two cousins, Victoria and Florence Cochrane, who lived with Grandmama we much preferred Vicky, as we called her. Flo was absorbed in domestic affairs and was always a very bad last in the conversational race, almost an echo. Vicky was still attractive and must have been pretty in her youth. She used to sing us old French songs to a guitar, in a tiny voice. It was like a very old musical box and she herself a dainty but faded figure on it, turning her head from side to side as she played, with black hair dressed high on a cushion, and very bright, dark eyes. She was tiny and very upright, with the smallest hands I ever saw. Vicky might also be called a spinster by nature, though it is on record that a bold sailor once paid her attentions and, calling late one afternoon, was so rash as to propose. He was instantly refused, and left the house discomfited. The incident would have remained unknown to history but that poor Victoria was so overcome at his audacity that Mrs. Hamerston had to go to her assistance, and told Aunt Chatty that 'Miss Victoria was that angry, she clawed the air.' Florence I do not fancy had any romance, she was a kind old slow-coach given up to the material cares of life.

The dominant spirit in the house was undoubtedly Aunt Chatty. She was really clever, but her peculiar religious views no doubt gave a kink to her outlook on life. Instant conversion to holiness was the idea, and we were told the exact day, and even the hour, when many of her friends had found grace, with endless stories of wonderful awakenings – after which no further efforts to keep in the narrow way seemed necessary. Often she would tell us, 'I am on the Rock', with complete satisfaction as though she alone occupied that supreme position and all others were wallowing in unrighteousness and wrath to come. Those who did not share these narrow views were swept off the board, labelled wicked and worldly. 'Judge not that ye be not judged' had no place in this creed. It was all very puzzling, especially as in poor Aunt Chatty's case it was combined with great elasticity of conscience that had much affinity to humbug. Fate had decreed she and Grandmama must live together, but I do not think they really were in unison. Aunt Chatty had an odd habit of playing little tricks on Grandmama that surprised our young minds.

Once I was made to dress up as a queer poor little woman come to beg, wearing a frowsy old shawl and bonnet, and trailing skirt, much disliking the role forced on me. Then, armed with a forged letter from Baptist Noel, recommending this poor person to Grandmama's charity, I had an interview with her, in a dark room one evening. I stood with my back to the light as she sailed in, my heart in my mouth, but Grandmama merely said what she would describe as 'a few kind words' to the poor woman. 'Are you a good Christian?' she began, 'Do you read your Bible?' 'Do you attend Chapel?' To each question I answered nervously, 'Oh, yes, milady', with a sob, and wondered what more was expected of me. But Grandmama seemed satisfied and only added, 'As Mr. Noel says, you are a very deserving person, here are some tracts which I hope you will read, and here are five shillings – Good night.' The 'deserving person', feeling rather ashamed of Grandmama's kindness, retired from the scene to Aunt Chatty, who was listening at the door, shaking with laughter. 'Capital, dear child,' she said, 'Capital.' I felt depressed and thought the five shillings too good to be true and resolved to return them to Grandmama.

Next day, at luncheon, Aunt Chatty said, slyly, 'I wonder what that poor woman is doing today.' Grandmama, at once wishing to improve the occasion, said mournfully, 'I am afraid she is not having so good a dinner as we are, poor creature.' 'Indeed, Mama' said my aunt, nodding mysteriously, 'I believe she is having very much the same.' 'What do you mean, Charlotte?', asked Grandmama in a puzzled way. 'Ah ha, Mama', Chatty proclaimed triumphantly, 'it was not a poor person at all, it was Laura, dressed up!' How would Grandmama take it? I was frightened lest she should be angry with me, and well remember the relief when she held out her hand to me and said, smiling, 'Laura, was it indeed? Come and kiss me, dear child, it was very clever of you to take me in.' Screwing up my courage, I went to her side and kissed her, saying, 'Here are the five shillings you gave me, Grandmama,' putting the two precious half crowns on the table beside her. Like music was her quick reply, 'No, no, dear child, keep it – it is for you, for such a good piece of acting.'

I remember half of this unexpected addition of fortune to our weekly dole of twopence was spent on a long cherished project of having our two darling dolls photographed at a real photographer's. We went next day to 'the Grove', a cheap place; we had rehearsed many life-like groups for this picture, but the man was grumpy and would only photograph our dear wax children if we left them with him till next day. When the longed-for photograph came we nearly wept, for he had done them just stuck up against a table, one standing, one sitting, looking as Vi and I said sadly to each other 'just like dolls', which perhaps was not as odd as we thought it.

If Aunt Chatty used to play tricks on Grandmama, she in her way used to tease Aunt Chatty, who was inclined to *embonpoint*, not to say fat, and sometimes banted in a half-hearted sort of way. At luncheon Grandmama would say to the butler, with an abstracted, holy air, 'Barlow, do not hand the potatoes to Miss Charlotte, they are not good for her.' Chatty rose like a fish, 'Indeed, Mama, I will eat potatoes if I like – Barlow, hand me the potatoes directly.' The poor man, having withdrawn to the sideboard with the dish at Grandmama's order, now lurched forward to offer them to my aunt. 'Barlow,' Grandmama said firmly, 'do not hand the potatoes to Miss Charlotte.' Barlow hesitated halfway, Chatty with rising anger ordered, 'I will have the potatoes. Barlow, hand them me at once.' Grandmama stood firm in her resolve, 'Barlow, I forbid you to hand the potatoes to Miss Charlotte.' My poor aunt, waxing hot and red, said sternly, with an imperious wave of her hand, 'Barlow, I *command* you to hand me the potatoes.' What was the poor wretch to do? He chose the right, indeed the only course possible between the two angry ladies and, flinging the dish of potatoes on the table between them, hastily left the room.

These little altercations were the greatest surprise to our young minds, being far removed from any former experiences of grown-ups and their ways. Grandmama had a curious aversion to anyone knowing her age. When the census was taken we were told she always hired a four wheel cab and drove about London all night, so that she was nowhere, as it were, and did not appear on the census paper at all.

I do not suppose we were sorry to leave for our dear home, Runcton, at the end of this visit. We only saw Grandmama once more, and that most unexpectedly. One everyday afternoon, in our Runcton school-room, all deep in lessons and eager for any diversion, we spied a fly slowly crawling up the Approach. Who could it be? No one ever called without notice. Three heads were pressed to the window. Amy said, lightly drawing a bow at a venture, 'I should think it was Grandmama and Aunt Chatty.' We all laughed, but it was! A few minutes later the butler threw open the school-room door and announced, 'Your Grandmama, young ladies.' Nothing so surprising had ever happened to us. Grandmama sailed in, in her usual sable trappings and her faint smile. It appeared Aunt Chatty was in Lynn, our small market town, where they had taken lodgings, wishing to pay us a surprise visit. We drove in next day to see them, in a tiny, teeny house near the Lynn Gates. But Grandpapa was so vexed in his hospitable soul he would not allow them to remain there, insisting quite rightly on their joining us at Runcton. They arrived next day, but I do not think the visit was a great success. Aunt Chatty at once took to her bed with neuralgia, or was it shyness? She told us she slept with twelve yards of flannel round her head, enough to make anyone ill. Grandmama was not happy either, staying with the relations whom she and Aunt Chatty used to call 'those worldly Gurneys'. I think they left very soon. I remember Grandmama at breakfast saying, 'How grass the green is, Mr. Gurney' repeatedly, and buttering her toast both sides by mistake.

Grandmama died rather suddenly, the mystery of her age still kept up. She had a paralytic stroke and was quickly at rest. There is a quaint letter from my brother Tom on the subject, showing rather mixed feelings . . . *how awfully sad Grandmama being dead — but how awfully jolly if you come up for the funeral, you simply must.* Poor Chatty was now alone, but for the cousins who made their home with her. We stayed with them once while they were still in Queen's Gardens, and Chatty took us to hear Moody and Sankey at a big Revivalist meeting. It was a long expedition in a growler. On the way a cab horse, from another cab, put his head in at the window and Aunt Chatty declared it was Satan himself! The meeting was very long and quite incomprehensible to us. But I seem to remember that this visit was more cheerful, and Chatty never read us Commentaries, though she was fond of asking searching questions about one's soul – very disconcerting to the young.

She was interested in our love of drawing and took us to see pictures at the South Kensington Museum. The following year she migrated to Netherwood Road, Shepherd's Bush – a most dreary suburb of London, then only to be got at by the Underground Railway, which was a sort of smoky inferno in those days. The house was a dull little villa, bounded on all sides by brick fields and half built box-like houses, all pin for pin alike, and sad to see green spaces swallowed up by such mean streets. Here Chatty gathered round her a sort of frumpish court of female friends of pronounced Evangelical views and curious appearance. Miss Jolly, an ex-school mistress, buxom and jet-covered; and Miss Andrews, a gaunt creature like a man dressed as a woman, in a long raw umber cloak. I think she was an artist and helped my aunt with the sixteen portraits and busts of Mr. Baptist Noel she painted after his death. Miss Beamish, very melancholy; Miss Taylor, very gushing, who called us 'the glorious little Trio' and sang hymns constantly in a windy voice, accompanying herself on the piano with one finger. She was especially grovelling to Chatty. The one we liked best was a Miss Kinnaird, she was a Swedenborgian, so we were told but had not the faintest idea of what it meant. They often had religious arguments, when Miss Kinnaird would talk volubly of the 'Infinitesimal duct' (we thought she said 'duck', which made her conversation on religion still more mysterious), but we liked her because she sang to us, not Moody and Sankey revivalist hymns like Miss Taylor, but quaint old chants, also hymns to the Virgin Mary, of her own composition.

These visitors would either come to lunch and remain to tea, or arrive to tea and continue talking till supper time, when, merely untying their bonnet strings and throwing them back, they remained to share that odd meal of cocoa, sprats and cold, stewed, elderly gooseberries which was the usual menu – for gone were the days of plenty, flanked by Mrs. Hamerston and Barlow. At Netherwood Road a sterner régime had set in. At one time a mulatto cook used to hand in the *plats du jour* at the door, with a long brown hand and arm, showing no more ever of her dusky personality. Fortunately we were not greedy children and did not worry over these things, rather disgusting as they no doubt were. I think about this time our cousin Charles Walrond joined the party. He was clever and training to be a civil engineer. He lived on with them all their lives, they were devoted to him and he to them. There was much incense burnt at Aunt Chatty's shrine. Charles was very reserved and appeared to fit perfectly into that rather peculiar feminine household. They all went to Chapel together, and once we were taken to see a Baptist Total Immersion. It seemed to us most sordid and unattractive. After a good deal of extempore preaching some boards were removed from the centre of the floor, revealing a round tank of murky water. Down a step ladder the Minister descended, clothed in oilskins, followed one by one by a score of young women, dressed in flannel robes. These he took round the waist and ducked backwards, right under the water, swaying with their weight, saying 'I baptise thee Sarah', or otherwise. They came up gasping loudly for breath, there was no doubt that it was a total immersion. They scrambled from the unattractive pool and vanished into the vestry, leaving a dripping trail as they went. The men candidates were not allowed this luxury – they also wore mackintosh suits, like the Minister, but after the plunge had to return to their seats, where, with water pouring from their hair and beards, they dripped into tubs for the remainder of the service. All the while the crowded congregation stood up in their seats and climbed on the window ledges to see this sight. There did not seem any reverence or beauty, and indeed it was very far removed from the scenes on the banks of the Jordan, appearing to be an ugly travesty of those primitive and spiritual baptismal rites. Chatty told us Mr. Baptist Noel had immersed her in this way, in a tank, but that Grandmama was let off on account of her age.

Victoria [her cousin] suffered from a nervous dread of tunnels, so they could only go to places reached by coach, such as Richmond, or Brighton, for their summer holiday. Chatty, on the contrary, became less eccentric as time went on, broader-minded and less severe in her judgements. (She finally left Shepherd's Bush and her satellites – all the 'dear, good, earnest Christians' – for Kensington.) We were often told as children of the marvellous 'direct answers' to prayers vouchsafed to Aunt Chatty. One striking instance we always remembered, though perhaps not as intended. When my father was made A.D.C. to the Queen, after the Crimean War, he wished Grandmama and my aunt to attend the next Drawing Room, and for the latter to be presented. This Chatty much dreaded, she told us, because she considered it a snare of the Evil One. Still, she could not refuse St. Vincent's request, so had her Court dress made – white silk with a train of red velvet – praying earnestly all the time that she might not go, that something might happen to save her from this terrible worldly occasion. 'And would you believe it, my dears, the direct answer was vouchsafed to me, for the very day before the Drawing Room I came out with the measles!' To us it appeared more as a punishment than a blessing, but tastes cannot be accounted for.

Gradually, as time passed, we became very fond of poor old Chatty, realising that it is possible to be attached to people without always seeing eye to eye with them, a truth harder to understand in early youth.

The Weekly Round

Monday, August 25th, 1873

I got up at about eight and dressed in a great hurry as I wanted to to say good-bye to Tardy, Aunt Maggie, Sybby and Betty [Orde cousins] who were going by the early train. After they were gone we had breakfast and had to dash down to prayers in the middle. At nine o'clock, after prayers, Vi did her music till ten when we did lessons till half past eleven. Exercises and French *participes* and that sort of thing – which I *hate*.

After that Reddie came, as he does every Monday, he is the music master and oh how I do loathe and disgust *him and his lesson*. He cannot play the least, but he *thinks* he does very well. I have him for an hour, and then I go out and Vi has him. I believe he is *the most detestable* man in the world and the most conceited. Besides thinking that he plays so beautifully he thinks he can do *everything else* equally well, he also teaches abominably and does not care how one plays. Sometimes he gets up and walks about in the middle, and in addition to all this he makes the most awful noises and has every horrible scent emptied on his handkerchief, and black curls. During his lesson I was nearly maddened and *longed* to *tear* out of the room. It is such a horrid bore that one cannot do that sort of thing and that all the time I was quietly playing I was *longing* to *thump* him and say 'Beast! Beast! Beast!' out loud. After his lesson was over I went and sat in the garden and wrote my journal, which I liked. Then I came in to dinner, which we have at half past one.

After dinner I had a sort of *squabble* with Amy, in which *I* was right, but *Amy* triumphed. We then prepared our lessons for the next day till past four. I then read my history in the downstairs sitting-room and afterwards I wrote my journal till tea-time. Helen (who is a most awful copier) remarked at dinner that she wished to keep a private journal, so we gave her a book and she began to write it. How ridiculous!

We spent the evening at Valleyfield, as it was Aunt Kitty's birthday (she was thirty-seven). We had rather a nice evening, although it was rather dull really, but I liked it somehow.

Tuesday, August 26th, 1873

Got up in good time. Mr. Baines came in the morning, he is the drawing master, a very mild man and rather a dreader, but he does not teach badly, although I hate his lesson because it lasts too long. But this morning I liked it very much, because he never came near me. I sat in the middle of the field in front of the house and sketched it. It was a great success, and put me in a thoroughly good mind. I read my history till dinner, *Tales of a Grandfather*, very interesting and not nearly so dull as most histories.

Lancer [Orde] came to luncheon, nice and has such good manners but no decision and that is very tiresome. After lunch we all got bags and satchels filled with biscuits, pears, cake and puffs, and Amy, Vi, Lancer, Tom, Ernest and I set out for a long field walk. We walked about four miles, right across the fens and jumped loads of ditches, and when we came to a very large one we made a bridge of our jumping poles and managed to scramble across, getting awfully wet. When we had walked a very long way we found ourselves at the Setch river, so we walked by the side of the river till we came to Setch bridge, we then got into a large barge we saw in the river and sat there and ate our tea, much to the astonishment of loads of village children who came and idiotically stared at us the whole time, as if we were a sort of *show*.

After we had eaten all our provisions we thought it would be so *tame* to walk home the same way as we came, so we had the wild idea of getting a boat and rowing part of the way home. We sent the boys to ask if we could hire any, but were told there were none to be got unless we went to ask Mr. Seppings to lend us his — but we wouldn't give up. So the boys (although we do not know

Mr. Seppings) went down to his brewery and asked. Mr. Seppings was out but Mr. Hall, the manager, a very nice man and very obliging, said 'yes, certainly', he would lend it to us, and we might take it down the river as far as we liked, and he would send a boy to tow us down and bring the boat back, which was very kind of him as we do not know him the least and I do not think he knew who we were. However, he was very attentive and had the boat mopped up for us and a sack brought for us to sit on.

At last we were fairly off, and although none of us could row except Lancer, we managed, with the help of the boy, to go about a mile. We would have gone further but we saw a storm coming up, so we wanted to make haste home. We got out and as we had no money (except a half sovereign) to give the boy, Tom gave him a very nice two-bladed knife, which I think he liked. It then began to *pour* with rain and, as we had no jackets and only thin cotton dresses which we put round our necks, we soon got *soaking* wet to the *skin*. It was so cold down my back, however I did not care much, although my feet were dripping too, from getting into two ditches and having torn a *large* hole in my boot directly we set out. But these were mere matters of detail and we were neither *cross* nor *bickering* and that was the great thing. It stopped raining a little time before we got home, which we did at seven o'clock, very hungry, wet, cold and draggle-tailed, but having thoroughly enjoyed ourselves.

Wednesday, August 27th, 1873

Went to the Baths – delightful as usual. We did not come home till twelve, when we did a few lessons till dinner-time. Afterwards I went downstairs with Helen to the sitting-room to draw. Found Vi and Ernest there and we all drew till about four, when Vi, Ernest and Helen went out, which I was rather glad of, because Ernest *would* keep bickering with Helen about foolish little things and contradicting whatever she said. I stayed in and drew till six, which I liked much. I was doing my Club drawing for this month, and as we have to send them next Saturday I thought I had better begin it. The subject was 'Rest', and I drew that picture of Master Lambton, sitting on the rocks, which after I had begun six times, I drew very well and it was a thorough success. I think I have a good deal of *plodding perseverence*, which I forgot to put in my description of my character. I also forgot to put that I am rather a coward (although I have presence of mind, I think), except in swimming when I have not the *least* fright and which I can do very well indeed.

But to return to my day, Amy and Clem went in the afternoon to call on Mrs. Wright, as she was out they went round the garden and bagged a peach and lots of mulberries! I wish I had been there. Tom and Ernest went to tea at the Rectory, so we had a peaceful tea, after which I drew again *all* the evening till suppertime, when Geoff [Gurney] whom the boys had brought home with them, went away. I think that boy is rather nicer than he used to be. After supper I drew again till ten, when I had *finished* my drawing, which I was so glad of. I forgot to put that yesterday when we came home from our walk, Lancer made a most awful *bourde* (*gaffe*) and told *Grandpapa* that we had tea in a barge near Setch and that idiot Stanbrook actually went to Grandpapa and had the impertinence to tell him that *we* had been going about jumping ditches and had taken loads of eatables and that Tom had gone without a jacket, and stirred up Grandpapa into making a thorough fuss, so of course this morning Grandpapa had 'a few words' with Clem and got into an awful rage about it. What would he say if he knew we had been down the river in a boat?

Thursday, August 28th, 1873

We six and Clem started by the nine train to go to Hunstanton for the day, with all the Valls [Valleyfield cousins], Uncle Tum and Aunt Kitty. We travelled third class and had great fun, as there were seventeen of us. When we arrived we walked along the top of the cliff to Old Hunstanton beach. As soon as we got there we hired five bathing machines and all bathed, it was so delightful. Uncle Tum and Wally had Norfolk jackets and trousers, they did look so funny. The sea was not the least rough, but it was a little too shallow, even when we went very far out. We stayed in some time, when we were dressed we had dinner on the beach, it was so jolly. We had pies and sausage rolls, buns and puffs and all sorts of things. After we had had a thoroughly good dinner we walked about on the beach and climbed the rocks. But it suddenly began to pour so we had to dash into the Inn and sit there for about a quarter of an hour in a very smelly room. However, we soon went out again and began dawdling slowly along the beach towards New Hunstanton. It poured twice before we got there, but we scurried under shelter of the cliff so it did not matter. I played my instrument (a sort of mouth organ) nearly the whole time. We wanted to have a quadrille on the sands, but we could not manage it.

Directly we got to Hunstanton it began to pour again so part of the time we spent at the station and part at Winlove's, where we had buns and ginger beer, till the four o'clock train, when we went back to Lynn. We played Russian Scandal in the train, which was very jolly. When we got home we had tea, as it was about six, then we had dessert with Grandpapa, which we do every night at seven. Afterwards I put the finishing touches to my drawing, and I then wrote my journal till bedtime.

Friday, August 29th, 1873

On this day, six years ago, darling Mama died. I thought a good deal about her in the morning. We told Helen all about dear Papa and Mama's death, which I liked, although it nearly made me cry. The boys went to the cricket match at the Towers, Amy practised, and Vi and I went and cleaned out the Den. All the afternoon we were *slaving* at it, dusting and washing disgustingly dirty crockery and stewing mulberries until we were thoroughly tired of it. When the boys came in at about five they went with Amy into the Den and began vaguely cooking and pulling the things about. I read *Daring Deeds* but I did not really enjoy it because I was thinking secretly all the time that I *ought* to be finishing my music, and that Mama would like me to do it.

I read that dreader book all the evening, which was very unsatisfactory somehow.

Saturday, August 30th, 1873

Got up rather late and had a normal breakfast. I do not mean things to eat, but that there was nothing but discussions, arguments and bickerings going on the whole time, principally between Amy and Ernest, as they were both in bad minds, and *all* about the *eatables*, which is so dreadful. After breakfast, after about an hour of *endless* discussions, Vi and I began to learn our lessons for Monday, which we always do on Saturday mornings. We finished at about eleven-thirty, and some of us drove into Lynn to have Ernest photographed in the little old hunting coat that belonged to Papa, when he was about six. Ernest was in a very good mind and looked such an *angel* in the coat.

After dinner Amy, Vi and I dressed to go to a croquet party at Mr. Bagg's, and called for Rosy and Lily on our way. We hated going as we had never seen any of the family before and they are all old. Mr. Bagg, the father, is rather a jolly old man, but Miss Bagg is a fiendish old maid, very chickenish and dreader. Mr. and Mrs. Edward Bagg were there, Captain Bagg, a Mr. Helsman, a dreader, and his son and daughter. We played *croquet* the *whole* time. Of course, to make it *better*, Amy (as usual) *forgot* to order the bus, so we were there a whole hour and a half more than we need have been. We did not get back till seven, as we took Rosy and Lily back to Valleyfield, where we found Connie [Gurney], who is staying there till Monday. She is thinner than she used to be, but is very plain, though she has a very kind face. Uncle Tum dined, but we happily did not have a drawing-room evening. I drew all the evening.

Sunday, August 31st, 1873

A lovely day. I drew a cherub's head in the morning. We went to church at eleven. Reggie Vernon is staying at the Rectory for a few days, and for that reason we have not seen Eva the whole week. Her nose bled all the time in church, it must have been *such* a bore for her, she used ten pocket handkerchiefs! They walked home with us after church, Reggie Vernon was rather nicer, although I do not care for him at all. In the afternoon Eva's nose bled *again*, it was so silly of her to come to church after it had bled so much. After church Vi, Tom and I went in the park, mushrooming. We did not get many but Rover started a leveret and, after a long chase, he caught it and bit its inside out. I was so sorry for it but still I was rather glad Rover caught it although it was poaching. I drew all the evening, which I liked.

Tom was *in a heavenly* mind all day, I hardly ever knew him so nice, but *Ernest* was in a *very* bad mind, especially in the evening. At supper I never saw him behave so abominably. We four had chicken and they two had sausage rolls, which made Ernest *so* angry that, while I was quietly eating he suddenly got up, seized my chicken bone in his *hand*, *gnawed* a large bit out of it and threw it back on my plate. We were all perfectly *astounded* at him, and scolded him very much. I could not help saying twice, 'disgustingly vulgar infant!', which made him so angry and ashamed that he bolted out of the room and spent nearly all the evening sulking and sobbing in the sink (in the housemaid's cupboard) which he nearly always does, or used to do, when he is angry. I drew till bedtime.

It is now a week since I began this journal and I think it is *surprising* the amount of times I seem to have been in a bad mind and I think I have put down too many silly little things. In my description of us I quite forgot to put that we have a habit which is a *very* bad one for some things and *rather* a good one for others, of *abusing* our relations when they do things *we* don't like, and making ribald remarks about them. In the *boys* it is vulgar, for they carry it to an excess, but we do it in *comparative* moderation. It is a *bad* habit because it takes away any respect we *might* otherwise have for them and because the Bible says that we shall have to give account at the last day for every *idle* word; and it is *rather* a good one because it is a *vent* for our indignation and because it does *them* no harm whatever, as *of course* we only do it among ourselves and it is rather amusing for us and makes us laugh.

We also have *names* for some of our relations – Grandpapa we nearly always talk of as Grobee, Uncle Herbert and Aunt Bache (among ourselves) are Hubbub and Chyke, Aunt Maggie and Uncle Jimmy are Magotha and Jimotha, Aunt Chatty is Duchats, Aunt Amy and Uncle Willy are Ama and Bilus, and Uncle Tum and Aunt Kitty are Tumbo and Kitginx. *Of course* these names we never tell *anybody*, and we do not mean any *harm* by them, but only use them as *shorts*. I also forgot to put that we exaggerate awfully.

Uncle Herbert and Aunt Bache

Rachel, Daniel Gurney's second daughter, married the Rev. Herbert Jones. She was my mother's elder sister and they were devoted to each other. Aunt Bache often spoke of her to us and of the days when they were young together. My third name, Rachel, I have as her god-daughter. She and Uncle Herbert were two of our guardians, perhaps on that account they worried much over us and our doings. So when we were children we associated them with many of the hated rules that went forth to spoil our innocent pleasures. Indeed it was only in later years that we came to love and appreciate them. Looking back it seems to me the trouble was that they thought, perhaps not unnaturally, Clem (our governess) was too young to be in charge of us, and made constant efforts to send her away and give us an older governess, which we keenly resented. They did not know how we clung to her and she to us.

This uncle and aunt lived at Sculthorpe Rectory, near Fakenham. It was a large rambling house, with a garden full of flowers, peach trees and a big apple orchard. The really unusual feature of the house was the drawing-room, through an anteroom, with folding doors that opened simultaneously. It was a perfect oval, copied from a room in a palace at St. Petersburg. The walls and ceiling were painted in soft grey and white, with scarlet-lined bays, with blue Nankin china, books and old pictures. The furniture was covered in scarlet, the carpet black, with small stars of white at long intervals – a big fireplace at either end, and Aunt Bache's grand piano. She loved music and played constantly, with quick, light fingers. In one window was a big oval table, always ready prepared for drawing, which we found most inspiring. There was an organ in the anteroom which Uncle Herb played. He had been very handsome when he was young, and was called, in his college days, 'Archangel Jones'. Children have terribly keen sight at times and we did not think my uncle at all beautiful. I remember Vi asked Aunt Bache one day, quite innocently, what Uncle Herbert was like when they married. She answered, rather hastily, 'Exactly like he is now, he has not changed at all.' Now that my eyes are more or less opened I see it was charming she should think so – but then, I am afraid, we were only amused.

They had married very young, she at nineteen, he twenty-one, and had remained true lovers all their lives. Their tragedy was that the child who was born to them twelve years after their marriage, Bertram Theodore, only lived six years, and died of a rare and obscure disease of the brain. Time softened their grief, there was no feeling of sadness in the house. They were both optimistic and took a keen interest in many things. Aunt Bache had what I call the three best gifts, music, art and literature. She wrote clever articles for the *Quarterly*, and other magazines, besides sketching and illuminating most minutely, and had also her music. She had a really artistic mind, with that keen love of nature and the beautiful in life that, joined to the power of idealising facts, does much to keep age and dull care away.

Aunt Bache drove a pair of ponies very quickly and went long distances in her pony carriage, she was a very good whip. In winter the ponies, or rather small cobs, whirled her about in a miniature brougham, which could scarcely contain her and Uncle Herb. To see them both emerge from it was like conjuring made easy. My uncle was very quaint and original. He admired my aunt enormously and used to say, 'When I die, write on my tombstone – *here lies Herb, the husband of Mrs. Herbert Jones.*' He was adored by his flock, indeed they both were. She had a delightful soft voice, and used to visit the schools very often and plan little treats for the children. She had a lending library for them, which was unusual so long ago, and at Christmas there was a grand dispensation of iced gingerbread cakes, with pink sugar mice on top.

Uncle Herb was a quaint sight driving through the village in a cart with a mule, called Emma. He jogged along, his huge tall hat on the back of his head, his curly grey hair flowing below it over his coat collar. The children coming out of school would run to him and trot along, holding on to the sides of the car, Uncle Herb looking like a benevolent giant, singing with them and driving slowly for fear they should tumble or get hurt. His church was always full, he sang well, and played the organ if Aunt Bache was tired. The hymns were often composed by him and were full of intense enthusiasm and devotion.

I learnt a lesson of forbearance and gentleness from Aunt Bache I hope I have never quite forgotten. In the centre of her drawing-room, on two steps, was a life-size cupid in plaster holding up a great gold basket full of scarlet geraniums and ferns in pots. In a moment of great awkwardness I walked backwards on to it, and to my horror the whole thing fell over with a crash – the 'White Boy' as we called him, was broken into fragments, the flowers in their pots scattered and smashed. I was speechless and pale with fright and could only say, 'Oh, Aunt Bache – oh, Aunt Bache.' I shall never forget her perfect self-control and kind voice, as she said quite gently, 'Never mind, darling Laura, it was an accident, and I was really rather tired of the White Boy'. But this was only to comfort me, for on our next visit we found the poor White Boy beautifully mended and done up.

No memory of Sculthorpe could be complete without a word of the two wonderful old servants, William Skipper and Elizabeth Carmen, called Billy and Booba. In a sketch at Runcton of Aunt Bache and Uncle Herb driving off on their honeymoon in an open carriage and four, Billy and Booba – as their maid and valet, are both seated in the rumble of the carriage. They remained on in faithful service to the end of their lives, only surviving my uncle and aunt a very short time. William Skipper was deaf, but one of the best of servants and absolutely feudal. Booba reigned in the kitchen with an underling, she also waited on 'Aunt', as she called her, and made many of her dresses. She refused many offers, for she was an excellent cook and comely too. She used to tell us, laughing, she 'did not want the men'. One old parson, even, asked her to marry him, and we used to make her tell us the story of his courtship, which she did in her Norfolk dialect. 'Mr. Gale he say, "Mrs. Carmen, you're an' enchanten' woman – will ye marry me?"' She would answer, shaking her head, 'No, Sir, thank you, Sir – and I tell him to goo. I'll never leave Aunt – if she sent me away I'd only come back again.'

Although Booba remains in my mind as rather a comic personality she had a curious mystic side to her and used to dream strange dreams, to her they were visions. She once told us she had often seen our mother, to whom she was devoted, the first six months after her death, always sorrowful-looking and holding out her hands – but the night little Bertram died she saw my mother with the little boy clasped in her arms and a radiant smile on her face – after that she never saw her again.

A curious fact it was that though these two old servants were so devoted, Aunt Bache seemed to us entirely without consideration for either of them, and took all their service as a matter of course. They never resented this and really worshipped both her and my uncle who, in any difficulty always rang for William. Even when my aunt's velvet dress was found to be on fire, he rang and Billy promptly came and put it out! Old John Bell, the coachman, was also a humble worshipper. He used to sit in the back seat of the pony carriage, looking like a withered apple in livery, and scramble up and down to open the endless gates. Once she kept him waiting in the snow a very long while, when he was driving the brougham and she was paying a call, and said as she got into the carriage, 'I'm afraid I have kept you waiting a long time, John.' His frozen face flickered into a smile as he said, touching his hat, 'Please, Ma'am, that's what I'm here for, Ma'am.' That was the spirit of their service – *altri tempi, altri mori.*

My uncle smoked strong cigars, the whole house smelt of them, faintly below, tempered with the breezes from the garden, but strengthening as you mounted the stairs to his study, where the full and appalling bouquet hung heavy and never to be forgotten. He and Aunt Bache used to walk up and down the terrace, arm in arm, for hours, in endless and harmonious tête-à-tête, and I fancy, in the gloaming, their spirits might still be seen there, for they dearly loved Sculthorpe. He always wore a tall hat and a dark grey suit, and in winter a cloth cape over two or three greatcoats, but Aunt Bache dressed in youthful fashion, with her hair in curls.

Uncle Herb's brother, Sir Willoughby Jones, lived with his wife and children at Cranmer Hall, a big place close by. Our winter visits to Sculthorpe for theatricals, and the Cranmer dances, were some of our most joyful occasions. When we stayed there we usually danced (often a dance to which Aunt Bache would gallop, with one of us clinging to her) through the ante-room to the dining-room, when old Billy announced dinner. Sometimes Uncle Herb also joined in the dance, singing and laughing. Winter or summer we had an unfailing welcome at Sculthorpe.

Country Pastimes

Wednesday, September 16th, 1873 [to Sculthorpe]
We trimmed our hats in the morning. We, Amy and I, were both rather cross, *me* because my beautiful feather had not come and Amy because she wanted to have a blue feather. We started in the bus at eleven, the others went to the station with us. I was *so* sorry to leave *dear, dear* Runcton. I believe it is the nicest place in existence, it is so *peaceful* and free. We arrived at Fakenham at two and took a fly to Sculthorpe. Lawrence [Jones – Uncle Herb's nephew] came over from Cranmer, and we played croquet. It rained nearly all the time we were playing so at last we said we were sick of it, so went round the garden and ate peaches.

After he left we went up and dressed. Amy wore her black foulard, trimmed with white frills and a silver necklace and bracelets, while I had nothing but my old crumpled black muslin with white frills at the neck and sleeves. I did *bisque* so at not having a pretty gown. Altogether my toilette was very unsatisfactory as Stanbrook having left my sash behind I had to wear an old shred of Amy's. She had also left behind one of my arm ribbons and, to finish up, had left my right shoe at Runcton and brought Vi's left instead, which was of course very uncomfortable on my right foot! So I had a sort of consciousness of being wretchedly dressed, which prevented me thoroughly enjoying myself, and poor Amy on her part had the ghost of a headache the *whole* time. . . . At the dance I was not introduced to a single person, except a stupid old parson who bored me awfully and danced with me twice. I also danced once with that idiot Holway. I danced four times with L. [Lawrence], he is, with the exception of Mort, the worst dancer I ever saw. I strongly advised him to have some lessons, as he has never had any.

Thursday, September 17th, 1873

The much longed for wedding morning – [Lady Audrey Townshend to the Hon. Greville Howard, 2nd son of the 17th Earl of Suffolk]. I shall begin by telling you what we all wore. Amy and I had white nansook gowns, two large flounces on the underskirt, a very pretty polonaise of the same, trimmed with insertion with sky blue ribbon run through and lace on both sides. The bodies were made crossing over, we had capes to match, also trimmed, sky blue sashes, snoods and neck ribbons, white straw hats, very high crowns and with large round brims, trimmed with black grosgrain and white feathers, (Amy's had also a little blue one, and mine had a lovely pale blue rose). This, with primrose kid gloves, completed our costumes. I think we were very 'tweetly' dressed, don't you? Stanbrook said we looked 'quite lovely'! I forgot to put we had silver ornaments, white tulle ties, black silk stockings and high kid boots.

We started at about ten, Amy, I, Jimotha and Herbert in a fly, and Aunt Bache (who wore a dark red silk dress trimmed with black lace, and a cream colour bonnet covered with lace and pearls), – she looked very well indeed, and Aunt Maggie (who wore a very ugly dress, a light brown silk gown trimmed with dark brown silk, a white hairy stuff, with silk stripes, polonaise with no sleeves – which suited her very badly indeed – and a peacock grosgrain and white lace bonnet) went in the brougham. We arrived at the church at eleven and had excellent places in the chancel.

There we waited for about half an hour, and while we are waiting I will tell you a few toilettes – Lady Booba [Lady Elizabeth St. Aubyn, later Lady St. Levan], sister to the bride, had on a dark blue satin trimmed with light blue velvet. Lady Bute, who is lovely, quite tiny, with the most exquisite little figure, had a grena [dark carbuncle red] silk dress, trimmed with salmon colour silk. Aunt Kitty, who looked very nice indeed, had a maroon satin dress, quite plain, with a very long train and a pouffe bonnet to match and a good deal of white lace about her neck. Freda Cresswell had, as usual, a grey silk gown trimmed with pink. Little Eva North was there and looked very pretty in rose colour and white. The bridesmaids wore pale blue silk trimmed with gauze flounces of the same colour, and silk bows edged with dark grena velvet, long grena velvets round their necks and blue silk stockings and boots with rosettes. The five big ones had blue and grena bonnets, while the three little St. Aubyn girls had white straw hats, high and large-brimmed, lined with blue silk, caught up at one side with blue silk and blue and grena feathers. The five elder ones had silver bracelets with Lady Audrey's initials on them, and the three little ones had lockets the same.

Lady Audrey wore a white satin gown, trimmed with Brussels lace, and a Brussels lace veil fastened with diamond stars, a diamond necklace and earrings, orange blossom in her hair, and a very large bouquet. She trembled dreadfully as she came up the aisle on Lord Bute's arm (who gave her away), followed by her eight bridesmaids. I did pity her so, she did look so *agitée*. Everybody, of course, was staring at her. *Save* me from ever having a grand wedding. If ever I am married I should like to have nobody there but the clergyman and the bridegroom, and that reminds me of Mr. Howard, whom I have not spoken of yet. He looks rather old and stern, very like a surgeon, and not nearly good enough for her.

The ceremony was very impressive, it made one feel somehow what a very solemn thing marriage is. Soon after the service we walked up to the house [Raynham] and went into the Saloon, but there was such a crush there that we could not stay . . . The breakfast, which was in the large Hall, was very good indeed.

Lord Bute proposed the health of the bride and bridegroom and Mr. Howard returned thanks, but they neither of them made speeches. For going away Lady A. had on a dark blue velvet gown with a very long train, but as she came to the door her maid threw over her shoulders a splendid Indian shawl, red embroidered all over with gold, which was a wedding present from Lord Bute and had, so L. told me, cost £400, but it made her look rather old and prevented us seeing her gown. They drove off in a regular shower of flowers and old satin slippers (one of which went straight into the bridegroom's hat as he was taking it off to bow). Everybody then said good-bye and drove off, and so ended the much longed for wedding day. L. came down to say good-bye to us as he is going early tomorrow morning, to my great *bisquation*, for he is such a jolly boy. However we said good-bye six times!

Tuesday, September 22nd, 1873

In the evening we dined at Cranmer, at least Amy, Aunt Bache, Aunt Louisa and Uncle Herbert did, but I went early and had tea with them, which was much jollier as the dinner lasted nearly two hours. We played fortunes and Bank and Truth in the school-room.

Wednesday, September 23rd, 1873

We met the Jones girls in the summer-house and went for a walk with them which was jolly. We had a splendid idea of Amy and Mary dressing up as beggars and going to the Cranmer Farm for bread. Of course we talked it all over, how they are to be dressed and what they are to say.

Friday, October 2nd, 1873

Amy and I settled in the morning that we would do the Tramps today. So we ransacked the whole house for awful old things, of which we got a splendid stock from the maids. These we rolled up in one of our red cloaks and drove over to Cranmer in the 'car' with them. We drove into the Park as Amy wanted to sketch. The Joneses came out to meet us and thoroughly entered (in a Jonesish way, of course) into the Tramps. The time before lunch was spent in routing out more old things for the Tramps to wear and settling what they were to do and say. I forgot to say we had invited ourselves to luncheon.

After lunch they went up and dressed. Amy wore a filthy, holey, old grey petticoat, which we had damped and then rubbed on the leads, a sort of sick-coloured shawl over her shoulders and a smaller ditto over her head. These, with darkened eyebrows and false dark hair, thin naked arms and *horrible* filthy old boots, full of holes, that had been gnawed by rats, completed her costume. Mary [Jones] wore an ancient striped petticoat and then an ancient mohairy sort of dress over, and much shorter, which had a very *Trampish* effect, a light, thin sickly grey jacket with *mud-coloured* spots, a dirty duster round her neck and a *fearful* old hat, with a draggle-tailed purple feather in it poked up on one side of her head, a large red spotted handkerchief tied round her face for the toothache, a dark chignon and dark hair straggling out in front, which, as she has *really* very fair hair disguised her a good deal. On her legs were disgusting old *rucked* stockings that had *once* been white and awful old boots. I never saw such a couple of horrible old starved Tramps as they looked – *no more like Miss Troubridge* and *Miss Jones* than I am like my future *husband*, if ever I have one!

When they were dressed they came on to the lawn and we daubed *them* and their *dresses* all over with earth and water. They then set out for the Farm and we watched them from the nursery window, *slouching* across the Park. They went to the Farm and utterly took in old Mrs. Stubbs, who gave them horrible *lumps* of cold pudding and bread and butter. They afterwards went to Mrs. Barnes, the gardener's wife, and asked the way to a few places. She also was *utterly* taken in. Amy asked if Mr. Jones lived anywhere about here, but, on being directed she said she 'Would not go there, he was a hard man, a very hard man', which was rather *riche* [family word for amusing]. Soon after they came in and undressed and then we drove home. On the whole it was decidedly *slow*, as everything that has to do with Cranmer (except when L. is at home) always is. We heard afterwards, in a roundabout way, that the strange Tramps had attracted a great deal of attention, and Mrs. Barnes' opinion was 'that the tall one had evidently seen better days, poor thing.'

Thursday, October 8th, 1873

Miss Marsh arrived. She is very kind and nice and rather amusing, though a great chatterbox. She also teaches well, I think. We are both learning Italian with her, which I like very much.

Saturday I spent almost entirely in the church drawing, in a very pre-Raphaeliteish way with a gold leaf background, a head out of the large church window. I finished *The Newcomes* in the evening, a most delightful book, though on the whole not satisfactory. I always like a book better when the people are unhappy in the beginning and happy in the middle and end, than when they begin happily and slowly sink into unhappiness and only recover quite at the end of the book. Tuesday morning we came home, after having been tipped ten shillings each by Uncle Herb. We found them all quite well and very glad to see us again, as we were them.

[Back at Runcton.]

This is how we spend our days now. We get up irregularly and breakfast ditto, but that and prayers are generally over at nine-thirty, when Vi does her music till ten and I read history and work. At ten Vi and I do an exercise or translation with Clem till eleven, while Amy does Italian downstairs with Miss Marsh. At eleven we have luncheon of cake and fruit and then we go for a tramp till twelve when we all come in, Helen to Orton, Amy to Italian upstairs, and Vi and I to Italian downstairs with Miss Marsh till one-thirty when we come up and have dinner, after which Amy practises in the drawing-room and I in the school-room till three, when we go another tramp till four. At four we all Italianise and literaturise with Miss Marsh downstairs till five-thirty, when we have finished lessons for the day and come up and have tea. After tea I either read or draw till seven, when we go down to dessert and afterwards I devote all my time, both before and after supper, which we have at eight, to working for the Christmas Tree for the village school children.

This plan of our days, which are all alike, will show that except on Saturday, which is a half-holiday, we have no time for painting, as we can only etch after tea by candlelight.

Thursday, October 22nd, 1873

We got up very late, at eight-thirty, and after prayers Vi, Eva,

Helen and I went to the kitchen to order Vi's birthday dinner. She ordered oysters, which as you know I *hate*, chicken and Peters [a kind of Genoese pastry]. Afterwards I spent all the morning till eleven-thirty hunting for something to copy for 'Holiday' for the Club, which I did at last find in the shape of that picture of *Children at Play* by Poussin, which I am going to paint in a pre-Raphaelite style.

Monday, October 26th, 1873

I was thinking the other day how I should spend my day if I was allowed to do as I liked and if it was possible. First I should get up whenever I felt inclined, then I would do *no* lessons all day (except perhaps sometimes read a little history), but I would not be *idle* – on the contrary, *very* industrious, for I should *draw all day long* and when I was sick of it, I should get a comfortable armchair by the fire and read a novel.

For *exercise* I should have a sort of double velocipede, consisting of two armchairs, worked either by hand or foot, which would go about a *hundred* or *fifty* miles an hour. But I should always have the second armchair filled by somebody who I *really* wanted to drive with me and I should like to have the power of wishing any person to be in it I wanted. (I know who would be there *very* often), and we would go long drives about, spinning along, almost like flying. In the evening we would either take a long *moonlight* drive or else go to a *dance* or the play, whichever we felt inclined for. I should *always* have *loads* of money and *loads* of new novels. I should *always* be *exquisitely* dressed and *never* wear old *slonche fouffes* [family word for clothes], and should *also* have hair over my forehead! I forgot to put I should be *awfully* kind and should always be giving everybody heaps of splendid presents.

Would not that be a delightful life? I forgot to put I should very often travel, always with my velocipede and my companion and I should also sometimes go to London, the two last of course with the others too, who I should be awfully jolly to and who would adore me.

On Wednesday morning we went to see Jemima Palgrave and John James Taylor married in this church. Jemima is Ellen, the housemaid's, sister. The only people there were Baxter [the Clerk], Mrs. Crisp and niece, Stanbrook, us five and Miss Marsh, Mr. Eller, who married them, and the bridal party which consisted of the bridegroom, who is a blacksmith and very ugly, the bride, who wore a grey silk gown, a white cape and a white tulle bonnet with orange blossom, in which she looked very nice, as she is tall and slim, one bridesmaid, who wore a green silk gown, striped with yellow, a white cape and bonnet and a scarlet face, and George Palgrave, who gave away the bride, in his Sunday clothes and grinning from *ear to ear* the *whole* time.

These four stood in a row at the altar, which made it look exactly like a *double* wedding – but the ceremony went off very well indeed except that the man said 'Yes, Sir' instead of 'I will' which made Amy and I explode. The bride was *very* composed and self-possessed and did not even tremble, in fact she blew her nose twice *loudly* during the ceremony. This and G.P.'s. grin greatly took off from the *solemnity*. As they walked down the aisle Amy wanted very much to play the *Wedding March*, but unfortunately she had never played on that organ so did not dare try without having practised it, for it would have been so *extremely* dreader to have played one or two weak notes and then broken down, but it would have been rather *riche* if she could have done it. When they, the happy pair, came out they were rather weakly pelted with rice and one or two old slippers, which were *instantly* picked up and restored to their owners by an excited villager. We heard the bells vaguely clashing, in a most hideous weak way, invented, I suppose, by Baxter. Altogether it was not an *impressive* affair, *rather* different from the last wedding we were at!

I finished *Frank Lawrence* before dessert. I like it *awfully* although I think the people were all *idiots*, but then if they had not been there would have been no story. It is *extraordinary* how interested one does get in some books and how thoroughly one *lives* with the characters and is *happy* when *they* are *happy* and *sad* when *they* are *sad* and how much one is affected, at least I am, by the deaths of either the hero or heroine. Oh, I do like a book that ends satisfactorily, by *that* I mean when the hero and heroine, after many troubles, marry comfortably off in the end and live happily ever after. Whereas in *Frank Lawrence* the hero and heroine, after an infinite amount of troubles and mistakes, that they might *quite* well have prevented if either of them had had the *least* common sense, end by being drowned (unmarried), locked in each other's arms, which is of course most affecting but *most* unsatisfactory. There is naturally a 'bookish beast' who is the cause of all these misfortunes and comes (as a matter of course) to a bad end, being dashed to pieces down a stone area, after having tried to burn a will and murder a man, and *that* (his death) is the only really satisfactory thing in the whole book.

Friday, October 30th, 1873

Our Gurney cousins, Cecil, Lovel, Edward and Hudson arrived to stay. In the afternoon we took Helen out in the dickey and Cecil rode Tip, who pulled dreadfully and ended by running away with him altogether. He galloped from Greenacres right down the road and banged open the yard gate, which was shut, and did not stop till he got into the stable yard, having frightened a horse which was on the road and made it run away. It (the horse) was in a gig with three people, a man and a woman in the front seat and another man in the back. The horse dashed into the hedge and tilted the gig up so that the hinder man *rolled* out, like a great *bale*. There they managed to stop the horse but they were all in an awful fright and looked as if they had never driven before in their lives, the woman was nearly crying. Of course we went up to them and hoped they were not hurt etc. etc., but they were highly indignant.

Edward, who is seven, came and dressed me in the evening, he was such a darling, being my maid and tying all my bows. How I should like to have a child like him. He is so *awfully* angelic, he looks as if he *could* not do anything wrong, almost too good to live. They are all of them great darlings, but so tiresome sometimes. For instance, yesterday afternoon they all got hold of the instruments and there was Lovel playing on the Shepherd's reed, drum and penny whistle, Cecil on the fiddle, Edward on the accordion and Amy learning a hymn on the piano – *all at once* for half an hour, at the end of which time I was reduced to a state *bordering* on INSANITY!

It is so dreadful of me utterly to forget to put anything about Uncle Walrond's death, which we heard of today. He went to Yarmouth, with a friend of his, they went to the Star Inn to sleep and he was found dead the next morning, it is supposed of apoplexy. Oh how awful for his children, I *am* so sorry for them, poor, poor things. I should think they could hardly believe it. It seems too extraordinary to think that that man we saw in London this summer is *now seeing* Mama and Papa in Heaven, I wonder if he told them he had seen us. How glad he must be and how happy to be with Aunt Louisa and his other wife. [Theodore Walrond was a widower when he married Louisa Troubridge.]

November 23rd, 1873

As nothing particular happened today I will write a few vague sentences about different things. We began fires about a week ago, they *are* so delicious. How I wish I could give every poor person coals for the whole winter, it must be so dreadful not to have one.

The water, which I believe I mentioned was perfectly *disgusting*, has at last by dint of incessant hackings at Grobee, been analysed, and to our *great* triumph one *tenth* of it was found to be *sewage*! I put 'triumph' because Grandpapa and all the servants declared the water did not taste and that it was only *our fancies*.

I think it is so nice to be in bed, although I think it is an awful bore to break up one's evening and to undress, but still, when one is in bed in winter it certainly is very nice. In summer it is much nicer I think to be out, because one is so awfully hot with blankets on and when one has nothing but the sheet I think it is worse. I do like having something awfully heavy on. When I was in

London and it was so very hot I always had a sheet and on the top of that a large oil painting without a frame, very heavy and just the size of my bed, so it made a very good counterpane. But now it is so delicious to be warm and one gets so awfully comfortable. One can think so delightfully in bed, there is no fear of being interrupted and my thoughts never come so quickly as when I am in bed. Then I make plans and castles in the air without end, all sorts, and scenes and conversations and events in my future life. Then it is such fun one feels exactly as if one was doing the things and it is almost as much fun as if one was.

Another thing I think *awfully* nice which has to do with beds and that is dreaming, especially when one remembers them in the morning. It is so *very curious* that one's brain should remain awake while one's body is asleep and that one should do and feel and say and see all sorts of things, just as if one was awake (only sometimes they are rather odd things). But what is so curious is that they are always in some way connected with one's real life. For instance, when I dream about Papa and Mama it is always that they have been dead and have come to life again, *never* that we are going on in the old way. But that is a dream I like so *very, very* much, it always makes me feel so glad and happy when I have dreamt about them, although they are sad too, for I always *beg* and *implore* them not to die in my dreams, and once I woke with, as I thought, my arms round Mama's neck, and I was *imploring* her to *promise* that she would *never, never* leave me any more, which made me sad when I woke.

I *never* have frightening dreams, I think only children have them. Once I looked in a dream book, that belongs to Clem, to see what a dream that I should *think* I have dreamt about twenty times means. The dream is that I am in great danger from cows (of which I am very much afraid), and it means that I have a very powerful rival – which is most ridiculous, of course I don't believe it.

December 6th, 1873

Amy rode with Rose Hutton, it is so odd that she, Amy, has suddenly got very keen about the Huttons' Fancy Ball, but she showed her keenness in such a characteristic way by saying, 'Oh, you know, it would be very easy to make up costumes for us – you and Vi might just go as peasants, or something or other, just with white caps and common stuffs, any old things would do, they would be very pretty, you know, with long plaits down your backs – and I might go as Dolly Varden, with a chintz gown very much *relevé* over a coloured, padded silk petticoat, which would not cost much, quite a common silk, you know, with a pretty little cap, it would be very jolly . . .' I say 'characteristic' because *we* might have 'any old stuff' and her *chintz* and *silk* would be new!

I went to bed in a *furious* state of mind, which Vi worked me up into by her going over everything about the Fancy Ball. In the first place Grandpapa has accepted, without ever telling us anything about it, *but* he has said he would *not* allow us to be dressed up, and we say we won't go at all unless we are in costume. Just imagine it, *everyone* else will be dressed up and of course looking their best, while *we* would be *dulling* in everyday clothes and skimpy old coiffures – *Thanks!*

Uncle Tum, Aunt Kitty and Rosy came to lunch next day. He was in the most *delightful* mind and says that he is going to *make* Grobee let us go dressed up as historical characters and he is coming up tomorrow morning on purpose. He got out books and found costumes for all of us. Amy is going as Marie Thérèse, the Princesse Royale, Vi is to be Charlotte Corday, and I am going as my great-grandmother, Catherine Bell, from the picture in the hall – so Gloriosa Calibosa!

December 11th, 1873

Tumbo came, he asked Grobee and this is the result – that if Major Hutton writes to G. to say he doesn't mind our not coming in costume, then we won't go in costume, but if the contrary, then G. will perhaps let us go dressed up. So in the afternoon

Clem and we three tramped to the Huttons, called on Rose and explained it all to her, telling her to make her Papa refuse to have us unless we are dressed up, which I think is rather stunning.

December 15th, 1873

All the Huttons came up here this afternoon to tell Grobee that they would not have us unless we were in costume and then to beg him to let us go. Is not it *stunning* of Rose? But how she dared do it I can't think. Grobee is so very odd, fancy he did not say a word about it to us, although he was in a very good mind when we went to bed.

December 21st and Christmas Eve, 1873

Uncle Tum came to lunch but was in an awfully un-usish mind and did not seem the least sorry that we are *not* to go to the Huttons' Ball, for Grobee has settled that we are not to go because we are too old to go alone with the boys, and he knows that the Huttons won't allow grown-ups. It *is* such bosh and we are all so angry and disappointed about it, for we all expected we were going. Really, I do think he *might* have let us go, it was not kind of him, was it?

But on Christmas Eve, instanter after dinner Amy and I did the most stunning thing, we went straight to Grobee and asked him if the Recs. [the cousins at the Rectory] might not some of them come in the evening as he had decreed they were not to dine. He said yes, directly, and by all means. However it really was *riche* of us for they certainly would not have come if we had not asked, but as it was the whole family, with the exception of Chenny, made their appearance after dinner. Tom, Ernest and I picked lots of holly and things and stuck them about the dining-room to give it a sort of festive appearance. They really looked rather nice, as we had a lump of holly and mistletoe in the middle of the room, which we have never been able to manage before. Tom had to stand on the mantelpiece and I supported him, standing on some steps, and Eva on the ground supported me, by which means we spasmodically hung it up.

We then went up to have a light tea, which for me consisted of lumps of gingerbread cake, a large one having just arrived from Scully. Vi, Eva and I then went to dress. I had, as I said, been very dull all day, but we all suddenly got jolly and felt we were going to have fun – which we did.

The dinner was stupid, of course, but the evening was awful fun. I danced every dance. Although there were so few people and it was of course rather weak, I enjoyed it much more than any other dance I have ever been at. Reggie Vernon, who is staying at the Rec., was there, he is not at all an acquirement, though, for he dances, valsing particularly, more abominably than anyone else I ever saw. *Even* worse than L. It is not his fault though, for he has never had any lessons.

We had a *Cotillon*, which I liked very much, as Wal, the best boy valser in the room, was my partner. We had a *Tempête*, the *Boulanger* and 'Wiss', altogether it was awfully jolly, only it left off *much* too early, at eleven-thirty. Was not it dreader? It ought to have gone on till two at least, don't you think so? But I must say I was rather tired and all because of my shoes, which being the most excruciating shape, with heels three inches high and toes an inch and a half wide, were not of the most comfortable sort. We wore, of course, our ancient of ancient blacks – and, oh, how sick I am of those *fouffes*. I had white holly and scarlet berries in my hair. We are one of the most uncomplimentary families I know, which is so nice, but, to give you an example of this, we were dancing the *Tempête* and as I came opposite to Amy and passed near her she said, 'How tweet you look!', which immediately put me in the most awful fright, for I thought my coiffure was coming down, or my gown coming off or something dreadful was happening to me or my dress, and went about asking everyone, but actually she really meant it!

The day after Christmas day was very dull. The afternoon we spent at the Huttons. Four mortal hours and a half – and what do you think we were doing all that time? Why, *sitting* in a *dark room* doing absolutely nothing! I never saw anything so badly managed in my life. In all that time there were only six Tableaux, they, in themselves, were very good, but *everyone* hated it and it was a *complete* failure, simply because they wasted such *hours* between each. They did not have half the programme, why it would have taken them till midnight. What idiots they were not to have music or something going on between the acts.

Saturday, Sunday and Monday nights it froze, so on Tuesday morning we all went down to the pond to look at the ice. It was great fun and awfully unsafe, we did not go on, but Tardy tucked his trousers up to his knees and we got a plank, one end of which we put on the ice and the other on land, and Tardy went down it and performed circus-ish antics on it and then ventured a little way off it on to the middle of the pond, the ice cracking all the time like fun. At last the boys got their skates and became much braver, in fact Tardy had a good skating morning, gliding grace-fully from one end to the other, while we stood on the bank and watched, dying to skate, but of course we could not, for the ice still cracked like mad and it would have been horrid if one of us had got in, although it did not matter for the boys. Tardy went on skating in the afternoon and got in, as it was thawing rapidly. He was only wet up to his waist, so he came in and changed directly and then went for a long walk to get warm.

I remember nothing else partic. that happened this week – the principal things were – but, oh, I forgot, I must speak about the Fancy Ball. Tardy and Lancer went, Tardy as Claude Duval, in a dress lent him by the Cresswells, which suited him very well, and Lancer in a uniform that Mort had when he was little, a volunteer's grey trimmed with green, rather ugly. Oh, how dull it was all that evening, and how we did long to go. I have not felt so disappointed for a long time.

Eleven people came here on their way, to show themselves – among them Gee in a very jolly red and gold uniform of Ozzie Cresswell's, with a long, false moustache, looking very nice. George Cresswell as an Algerian pirate, with enormous turban, huge black moustaches and wig, I did not know him the least when he came in, really his get-up was stunning, although he did (as R.V. remarked to me) look horribly wicked. Best of all was

73

Reggie Vernon, most beautifully dressed, as Don Juan. He had hired his dress of a London tailor for £3, and it certainly was lovely – but he smelt of onions! I had not to dance with him so I did not so much care and could examine his costume from a distance. It consisted of a high, emerald green hat trimmed with gold and a long white plume, a large ruff, short green velvet cloak, embroidered with gold, the body the same and also, I think, slashed with cherry colour satin, with which the cloak was lined, short puffed breeches to match and cherry colour silk stockings. He had a small false moustache and I never saw him look so well, really *awfully* handsome, which is a good deal for me to say, as you know I don't generally admire him.

Well, you can imagine how hard it was for us seeing all these people trooping off to the ball, while we were left moaning at home. Quite Cinderella-ish, only unfortunately minus the Fairy Godmother. Oh, how we did fume about it, Vi and I, I mean, for Amy and Jimotha had gone to spend the evening at Vall. to hear that darling Mr. Tready [George Treadcroft the tenor] sing. She had a middling evening as hardly anyone spoke to her.

Oh, dear, it is the last night of the year and instead of larking and dancing, dressed up at the Huttons', here we are dulling at home. Is not it enough to make a girl furious? Oh, dear, Oh, dear!

In pre-Raphaelite and Other Moods

January, 1874
Amy's present rage, which is shared by me, is to make her room
pre-Raphaelite, with a border of P.R. bulrushes all round it, the
pictures hung fresh and tied up with (as *she* says) beautiful grosgrain ribbon, but *really* dirty old snoods, and the grand thing of
all – a piece of black velvet, trimmed with black lace and covered
with really pretty (mostly done by me) P.R. paintings. Won't it
be tweet? All Saturday evening was taken up in drawing, painting,
inking, cutting out and velving bulrushes, for the bulrush part
is brown velvet and the rest painted. We all felt just like factory
girls, doing these different things so quickly.

Friday, January 9th, 1874
The day began hatefully by Grobee telling us that we were
not to go to the Cresswells' dance in powder, isn't it tiresome of
him? I ask you, now, what *possible* difference could it make to
him whether we went with black hair or white, and we *should*
have liked it so. However, it's no use thinking about it now, so
let's look cheerful – it will be all the same a hundred years hence.
I did not console myself with these reflections then, I was far too
bored and raved about it the *whole* morning, half laughing though,
not in a real rage, that would be far too much trouble.
In the afternoon, after heaps of deciding and *un*deciding, we
decided upon going to a dancing lesson at Vall. which Uncle
Tum, Freda and Edith [Cresswell] were going to give. We
thought it would be awfully dull but it really was rather jolly,
even *Amy* rather liked it, which for her was wonderful for she
never likes anything. I can't think why. She is most awfully
blasée, which she certainly has no right to be. What helped to
make her like it was that Freda told her she valsed well, which is

75

a good deal from Freda. It was so ridiculous, we were in fits of laughter the whole time, for they gave us lessons in deportment, for fun of course, which was too absurd. They went into ridiculous positions, to show us how we ought to stand and walk. We had a quadrille, Lancers and valse, and whatever we did badly they imitated, exaggerated of course, but so ridiculous it made one die to look at them, and was besides a very good way of teaching one, for it made one feel what a fool one must look.

Monday, January 12th, 1874

In the afternoon I painted the high heels of my white kid shoes sky blue and put blue bows on them. At seven we went to dress for the Cresswells' party, the much talked of 'Blue and White Dance'. We wore our white muslins with pale blue sashes and ribbons. When we were dressed lots of the servants came up to look at us, and Clem and Miss Marsh both said we all looked very much to our *advantage*, so let's hope we did. The absence of powder (forbidden by Grobee) did not prevent us from enjoying ourselves, for that we certainly *did* do, even *Amy*. I did not after all wear the shoes the heels of which I had painted so nicely, because, although they fitted they were rather short, and everyone told me what a torture high-heeled shoes are to dance in, so after deciding and undeciding for a long time and after a hard fight between *Vanity* and *Comfort Vanity* was *defeated* and my shoes remained at home. I certainly should have liked to have been powdered immensely; a good many people were, but most of them very badly. Uncle Tum told me he was exactly an hour, or more, over each of his girls' heads and that his nose was so full of violet powder he did not know what to do!

There were forty-six people and we kept it up till one. The music was very good, Mrs. Frost and a man who played sometimes on the triangle, sometimes on the trombone, and sometimes on the violin. I had several good valses.

Sculthorpe, January 14th, 1874

Laurence, [the son of Uncle Herb's brother, Sir Willoughby

Jones] came to lunch to talk over some charades they wish to have at Cranmer. He is just the same, only I think his face, I mean features, are getting larger and coarser, altogether he is rather lumbering and not handsome decidedly, although he is very nice-looking and all but six foot.

Runcton, January 26th, 1874

Those *darlingest, dearest, sweetest* boys went away on Friday. Those dear boys, it is such a bore, we do miss them so. It is perfectly *surprising* how they improve every holidays, they *were* so nice this time and *so* affectionate, also they are so *thoroughly us-ish* and jolly, and *really* I think their manners *have* rather improved. For instance, at meals they never *tear out* handfuls of new crumb bread, knead it up into squares of a quarter their original size with black hands, cut a *large* square of butter to put on top, for a chimney, and then *eat* it at *one* mouthful, as I have seen them do. Altogether they are *far* nicer and we had not *one* row, or even the *ghost* of one – so that I love them both more than I can say and am truly disgusted with myself for having written that *odious* description of them in the beginning of my journal.

February 19th, 1874

We went en famille to the Mart, which really was rather fun. Grandpapa gave us three shillings and sixpence each to buy 'Martings' with, Clem and Miss M. too. We all went to see some (as it was called outside) *Wonderful Performing Hares and Marvellous Clockwork Figures.* It was *too* wretched, it made one laugh because it was so awfully weak, but really I was almost *ashamed* to be there it was so *infantine.* The Marvellous Clock-work Figures consisted of little cardboard men which were drawn by wires slowly across the stage, one after the other, and a wretched man stood up and made a speech before each, telling what it was supposed to be. The Wonderful Performing Hares (of which there was a large painting outside representing a swell man in dress clothes, surrounded by a smiling audience in low gowns, showing off about twenty hares all doing different things such as dancing, playing the violin, jumping through hoops etc.) really consisted of one wretched half-starved animal that was brought in by a very dirty-looking man, a cross between a dilapidated gamekeeper and a respectable poacher which, when pulled with a string and told to 'drum for the Queen' gave a few spasmodic thumps on a weak tambourine. This went on for about twenty minutes, the only change being the altering of the names from the Queen to Prince Albert, the Prince of Wales, the Princess, the Royal Children etc., etc., till at last I thought they were going all through England, when they stopped and finished the performance by firing off a pistol which startled one out of one's senses and made a horrid smell of powder.

We did not go to any other shows except the *Living Skeleton*. Oh, he was so horrible, exactly like a skeleton – there was no deception at all. He was *sickening* to look at, pale yellow all over and his hands were scarlet. His joints were perfectly *enormous*, compared to the other parts of his arms and legs, they stuck out like great round lumps. His clothes were all padded, (I am glad to say he was quite dressed), for when George Cresswell went to see him three years ago, he had only a small petticoat on. His boots were also padded to prevent the *bones coming through the skin*, so the man who showed him off said. *Poor little wretch*, I should think he must die soon. I only *hope* they don't *starve* him. The man said he had very good health and ate and smoked tremendously. There were some doctors' certificates there of his good health, so I should think it is all right. There was a woman without arms to be seen, but we thought it would be too horrible so we did not go.

Oh, how I do *adore* Menier and Nougat chocolate, I think it is *heavenly*. How I wish I had a *vague* (admirer) who would send me *enormous* boxes full and how ill I should make myself with it. It is the only thing, except other sorts of choc. *and* ices, that I really *enjoy* eating. What I should *really* like to have would be, not a *vague* because that would be rather a bore, and also he might not think of sending me any, but to have *Miss Menier* (if there is such a person) for my greatest friend. What heaps of every kind of choc., but partic. nougat, I should make her fork out, wouldn't it be delightful?

Our evenings are so very jolly, for the plan is that Amy sings and plays the whole time and we draw and read. She sings so well, her voice is so pretty, the sort of thing one could listen to for hours and never get tired of and it is just the same with her playing. She can play absolutely everything and everything well, which is so delightful.

Saturday, February 28th, 1874

This was rather a jolly day, for we went to Lynn in the afternoon, the drive there was delicious, for it was a heavenly day. I only bought one thing for myself and what do you think it was? Why a *whole shilling's* worth of nougat chocolate! My dear girl, can you realise the *stravarth?* I have never done such a thing before, but this is how it happened – I had four shillings to spend, it was Drawing Club prize money, and I wished to buy one of the Household edition of Dickens' works, either four shillings bound or three shillings unbound. I was also thirsting for some choc., so I had a happy thought and ordered my book for three shillings (and directly it comes I shall send it to be bound and have it put down on Grobee's bill) which nice little arrangement gave me a shilling clear for nougat. Oh that I had it now, but alas it has departed this life.

Then Vi and Helen and I walked about Lynn hunting for a banjo, to give Tom for his birthday. We could not find one at Triven's and, as we had been there a long time, I was *obliged* to buy something, so I bought him a kite, which I knew he would hate. We then went to Street's, they had a banjo there, but it was a very good one and cost six shillings, so, as I had bought the kite, we could not afford it. We then went to Rix, to buy him a picture — there were nothing but very dreader enormous common ones, but as we had been giving such a lot of trouble I was obliged to buy a hideous picture called 'The Battle for the Standard', which he would also have hated. Vi then went to

Milbourne's and bought him a two shilling book called 'Windsor Castle'. I bought Rosy a present, as it was her birthday, of a draughtboard and men, one shilling and sixpence. When we got to the Livery stables Clem said our *achâts* were so wretched and Tom would *hate* them so that she *would* give them back to all the shops, get the money back and buy the banjo at Street's. So we drove round again to all the shops and Clem gave back the things and got the money. I wouldn't have dared do such a thing to save my life – but I was awfully glad we got the banjo all the same.

Our February half-holiday was very jolly for it came just in the strongest time of a new rage. It was for painting the panels of the shutters of our bedrooms, such fun to do; you can't think how pre-Raph. they look. Pale blue ground, oils – you know – quite grand, and in each panel droops a flower, of course very pre-Raphly done. The effect is stunning. I think that narcissus look almost the best, and they only take a jiffy to toss off. The rage held out, I'm glad to say, till we had done Amy's, and Clem's, the latter pale pink.

March 19th, 1874

Mr. and Mrs. Barclay and Ada arrived by the late train, Cousin Chennie more bouncing and bursting with kindness and good nature than ever. It was so dreadful of us that, having been rather hard up for jokes the last few days, we had made heaps of *awfully* weak ones about the Barclay Bounderbee's visit, for that is the *very* wretched name Amy gave them. I say it was dreadful because when they did come we had arrived at such a silly weak state that the mere sight of them *bounding* into the room, Cousin Chennie far fatter than ever, with three chins and an *enormous* crinny, sent us into fits of laughter. However they themselves are so awfully *bounding* and laughish, besides there being the natural *babel* of an arrival with everyone talking *very* loud at once, that it did not matter so much.

Friday, March 20th, 1874

Cousin C. *very* kindly took us all to Hunstanton for the day.

This is how it happened. She had never been there and wanted to see it very much, then she thought some of us would like to go too, and ended by taking A., H., V. and myself, which was very kind indeed and so like her. It was a *fearfully* windy day, we were nearly blown inside out going across the Green. However, the wind being at our backs we were happily blown into the Hotel, 'The Golden Lion', where we went first to order a sitting-room and a dinner of mutton chops and pancakes. We then went out for a walk on the pier, but finding that to keep our legs at all we had to cling on to the railings, and that if we stayed there a minute longer we should doubtless be blown into the sea, we thought we had better go back and try the cliff, which we accordingly did and found it, if possible, *worse*. Happily the wind was not towards the sea, so we were not blown over, but oh, our hats they were too maddening. We looked exactly like *drunk scaramouches*.

At last we were *obliged* to give up our walk in despair, so we all (with the exception of Cousin Chennie who bravely stumped on, holding on to an enormous umbrella nearly inside out) went back to the Hotel and arrived there perfectly exhausted. We sank down in the porch, where we remained perfectly immovable for half an hour, for you have no idea of the work it was to get there. It was just like cutting one's way through a cake of icy hard cold wind, and having one's ears boxed *hard* the whole time. At about one we saw Cousin C. labouring along in the distance, and when she came we were shown into rather a nice smelly sitting-room where the very first thing Cousin Bounderbee did was to bounce up to a large armchair and lump down in it, when it *immediately* smashed into atoms and they lay sprawling together on the floor, for Cousin C. was far too fat to get up. Oh, how we all *yelled*, she herself was in *fits* of laughter, it was too *riche* and so like her.

The chops, when they came, had the appearance of having been cooked with lots of grease and in a dirty pan, as I've no doubt they had, and the pancakes were exactly like leather *scarcely* eatable, but we were all perfectly *ravenous* and therefore did not care the least. But I had *visions* of those chops afterwards and I don't think I could have eaten them unless I had been sink-ing for food. After dinner as it was still blowing a gale we sent for a pack of cards and played games while Cousin Chennie went thumping about the town the whole afternoon.

There was rather a large dinner-party that evening – Ada had on rather a dreader black muslin, with black frills trimmed with white lace and red ribbons; we wore of course our black *pelures*. My evening was not so bad as usual for Tumbo and I had a long talk about the delights of India and the Tropics (at least that was the line he took) while I took the stay-at-home-dreadful-tigers-and-lions one, not the least because I *really* thought it, but be-cause it is much jollier in *that* sort of conversation if the people have different opinions. I liked it because he evidently liked talking with me and stayed about half an hour and then went away because he was obliged to, and said he never knew me so agreeable before.

I read the rest of the evening and finished that *heavenly Mill*. I don't believe I told you that I had bought George Eliot's *Mill on the Floss* the other day and have been plunged in it ever since. Oh, how I do *worship* that book, I really love Maggie and Stephen. Oh, the breathless excitement of their elopement and how awfully disappointing the chapter called 'Morning' is; she really *ought* to have married him, she had gone *far* too far to draw back and Philip and Lucy did not matter the least and Stephen was so *awfully* nice and far more interesting than that old hunchback who was, I am sure, hideous. It was very sad their dying, but under the circumstances I think it was the wisest thing they could have done and somehow or other although it was a flood that carried them off it was so well written it did not seem the least hackneyed. But, apart from the *Mill* it really amounts to absurdity how *dreadfully* hackneyed water accidents have become in books. If any river, particularly if it is subject to flooding, any pond, any sea, or in fact *any* water of *any* sort is mentioned in *any* book you may be quite certain there will be a drowning catastrophe of some sort or other before the book is out.

It is just the same about horses, if any animal is mentioned as being a shade less stolid than dickeys, there is *safe* to be an accident coming. In both cases it is generally the heroine who is the wretched victim and the hero comes out as the gallant preserver. But it is sometimes used as an easy way to kill off superfluous elderly relations. I have not read many books, but this is my experience and I find these two ways of thinning the characters far more popular than epidemics or fires, which are comparatively rare.

I went to stay at the Rectory with Eva for a few nights. In the first afternoon (it was a glorious day, exactly like summer) we took our books and sat outside their little house in the sun, reading and eating apples and nuts till tea; which was, I remember, rather meagre — consisting solely of marmalade and stale bread and butter. After, 'Beaver' and I dressed for the evening; I wore, of course, my black *pelure*, but I really felt *d'avoir l'air d'une reine* by the side of Beaver, who, poor dear, had on the most odious old *nipe* which had once belonged to one of her aunts and she had inherited unaltered, except made a little smaller. It was a foulard, a light ground with little scrimpy flowers on it, the body was tight and vilely ugly. She wore this polonaise over a light blue cotton skirt, with a *tiny, filthy, ancient* blue satin sash — even I felt less *typeuse*.

The evening downstairs was dull as usual, and we went to bed about ten. We had only just got into bed when we heard Aunt Ama come up to say good night. She was in her dressing-gown and looked too killing, exactly like those fat chinamen flying kites on Amy's Japanese screen, with two long plaits and a perfectly flat head. What do you think, every night she looks for robbers under Eva's bed, behind the curtains and in the wardrobe! I think that sort of thing is so stupid in one's own home; it is all very well at an hotel or in a strange place, but there it is too idiotic. Eva was in an awfully jolly talkish mind, but oh, how I had to pinch myself to keep awake. Several times I all but dropped off, but somehow I always managed to give the right answers, so I do not think Beaver twigged. I heard it strike, eleven, twelve, one, two and three, and then I really could not keep awake any longer.

The next morning I was, as I thought I should be, awfully tired and perfectly stiff – I suppose from sleeping on that iron bed. We got up at seven-thirty and breakfasted at eight. Oh, such a wretched meal – about five shreds of cold meat, shied on to a plate, a stale loaf and some butter, and that's all. The meat was not even in slices, but real scraps. I think it is so wrong of people to allow their children to have that sort of *horrible meagre* breakfast after they have not eaten for such a long time, and then go down and *gorge* themselves at all sorts of hot good things.

Eva had a holiday, so all the morning and all the afternoon we painted in their house. We settled that all the beams which mark out the house, are to be pale blue, with designs and patterns in pale colours on them, which harmonise very well with the yellow wood. Eva got some white oil paint, like painters use, from their gardener, and I fortunately had my oil paints with me, so we soon made a lovely colour, with which we painted, enjoying it very much.

Runcton Hall, April 11th, 1874

A few days ago we began painting the Den, we have now finished it and it is too delightful. Our rage for cooking having utterly gone, the Den had got into such a wild state of dirt and disorder, we really thought we ought to attend to it. So I had the happy thought of turning it into a studio and picture gallery, and painting the walls in a very pre-Raph. and artistic way, so we have. The walls are pale yellow, with a rather wide pale blue-green border, the two doors and the window frame are black, with blue and gold panels – it is so pretty. The tablecloth is maroon cloth and the bell-rope, which is too stunning and P.R., is maroon grosgrain wide ribbon. The pale yellow makes a very good ground for our pictures, of which we have already got a good many, all done by us of course. On the mantelpiece, which is covered with dark velvet, we have got a long row of our painted pots (the garden pots we had a rage for painting and decorating not long ago), and three rows more on a former bookshelf, now painted black. It looks so pretty with them on, the bright pots and the black together. On one part of the wall we have a large square of Moorish silk stuff, on which there are two black shelves with lots of really good china on them.

The principal chef d'oeuvre at present in the Den is a life-size oil painting of Ernest done by Amy. It is so good and very like, it really is very clever of her to have done it so well for she has never had a single lesson, or a single hint, about oil painting, which shows she must have great natural talent. When Uncle Tum saw it he said he thought it very like a rough Sir Joshua (Reynolds), which was the highest praise he could have given her, for it was exactly the style she aimed at.

Another great rage we had, and still have got, is for doing very P.R. oil paintings of Eastern people, they go by the name of 'Easternites', and are in the style of Alma Tadema's *Siesta*, from which we copied our first one. They are done on three things, either putty, cardboard or wood, all of which ways were thought of by me. I don't believe anyone ever painted on putty before. It is so jolly to do, you take a lump of putty, soften it with oil if required, then cover the surface of a board with gum thinly, then put with your thumb a thin layer of the putty all over the space required. It will be uneven, but you must then roll it with a small wooden roller. You can either outline your picture with a common pencil, or any pointed instrument, for no lead marks, but it indents a line wherever it touches. If you make a mistake you can smooth it out. You can then paint on it, as it takes any colour beautifully, you can also emboss any pattern you like on it by pressing down on to the soft putty anything with a raised pattern on it. In fact the whole thing is exactly like some ancient antediluvian painting out of the British Museum, and thoroughly satisfac.

One day of the holidays was *entirely* taken up, for me, with making a little old-fashioned frock for Helen. She is really an awfully clever twink [child] and is hardly ever naughty. It is so ridiculous how she catches up and uses our words and opinions and tries to copy us in everything, even in our rages. Whatever style for drawing is raging, you are sure to see rather weak and nearly *always* unfinished, attempts at it. Sometimes she draws *very* well indeed, but she has not much perseverance. About her frock, it is made of white muslin, two frills on the skirt, which is so narrow she can hardly bend in it, and reaches down to her ankles. The sleeves are short and puffed and so is the body which is very low-necked and with a waist just under her arms. Her hair has been cropped as short as a boy's and cut over her forehead, which *exactly* suits her.

I forgot to say when I was writing about the Den that Grobee kicked up the most awful row about it, took away all our paints, forbade us to go on with it and said it was to be papered at once – all of which would doubtless have happened if Clem had not angelically gone and talked to him and begged him for about half an hour, made him nearly relent and lugged him up to look at the Den (it was then nearly finished and quite neat), where he caught sight of Ernest's picture, just begun, which pleased him so that on the consideration that Amy could not go on with it without the paints, he quite relented and has taken an immense interest in the picture ever since, and has given Amy the present of a frame for it, which she is to order in Lynn.

April 14th, 1874

We spent the evening at Vall. and had great fun. We wore our dyed llamas for the first time, they are rather nice and very neat, not nearly so lumping as our gowns generally are, in fact rather sparse than otherwise, but with red sashes and ribbons and white frills, they really don't look at all bad.

April 17th, 1874

Imagine, Amy is going to Italy! For six weeks with Aunt Maggie and Uncle Jimmy [Orde], and Miss St. Quintin. You can fancy how astounded we were this morning when we heard. It seems too wonderful, we can hardly believe it and are in a wild state of excitement about it. When Amy dashed in, her face positively *bursting* with excitement, saying, 'I am going to Italy', of course we thought it was some wretched hoax, but she very soon convinced us, and in a few minutes everyone in the house knew the news. Oh, how delightful, and how I wish I was going too.

Colne House, Cromer, July 2nd, 1874 (Letter to Amy in London)
  Dearest Birma,
  *Oh the larkito − sharkito − of your London flauntings! What
fun they must be and what a stunning long letter you wrote me.
What heaven the Academy must have been, but I never heard of
Alma Tadema's* Moses, Overseer of Pharaoh's Granaries, *which
you said you had copied. I believe you mean* Joseph, *for I don't
think the other chap had anything to do with Pharaoh's eatables. Oh,
the opera! Oh, the Cowper Temples! In fact, Oh, everything. . . .*
  *Having now answered your letter I am going to launch forth into
a thorough description of our doings, which I can tell you are not to
be despised, yesterday being one of the jolliest days I have ever spent
away from home and at Colne House too. When we arrived the
first thing that met our eyes was Marie de Bunsen tearing to meet
us and Moritz playing croquet on the lawn. Oh the fun that girl is,
I don't know what we should do if she was not here. It is such a bore
that Moritz goes tomorrow, and Mr. Hubbard went this morning.
Oh, I forgot to say anything about him. He is a rather jolly man,
very keen about games and all that sort of thing, about twenty-two
and brother to Rose and Clemency. His name is Evelyn, he is quite
'Green Man' [best friends] with Moritz. In the morning Marie and
we three thought we would bathe, and Rachel [Buxton] said she
would come too. So we and Marie set off very early, leaving Rachel
to follow when they had had their 'pleasant little reading'! When
we got down to the beach we found Moritz and Mr. Hubbard just
going to set out fishing, so they persuaded us to go for a sail with
them − so in we dashed and off we went. Oh, what a lark it was,
everyone was laughing the whole time and it was so stunning to have
got off without any Buxtons. There was just enough wind to make
us sail very fast but not enough to make the sea the least rough − so
none of us had the slightest 'headache' (that is the proper way to
say you feel violently sick). We came back in about half an hour
for we knew Lady Buxton and Rachel were waiting for us. As it
was they came up fussing and Marie got rather a rowing for
having gone because, as Lady B. said, 'it was not in the plan'. Of*

course we did not care in the least but scurried off into our machine.

We had a most heavenly bathe, such a lark it was, we could all swim except Rachel, and there she was bobbing up and down, holding the rope, with the water about up to her knees, and there were we and Marie miles out, for Lady B. had sent a man and a boat to look after us as the current is so strong here, which was rather jolly, for then we could go right out of our depth and when we got tired let ourselves be towed in by a rope from the boat. After lunch we set off for a long drive, in four-in-hand dickeys. Oh, the fun that drive was — we had two carriages, sort of phaetons, with a box seat and another behind, all facing the horses, or rather the donkeys. Mr. Hubbard drove one and Viddy sat on the box beside him. Moritz drove the other and I went with him on the box. Neither of them had ever driven four-in-hand before but we had no accidents and did not smash into anything fortunately. I forgot to say that the back seats were filled up with Buxtons etc. Lady Buxton came in an enormous lumbering open carriage, bringing any who could not stuff into the other carriages, and also two fiendish females exactly like dilapidated scarecrows, the living image of each other. They looked exactly as if you had taken one frump, pressed it hard on the other and embossed a perfect copy. They both went by the name of Miss Fitch. Well, we drove to Beeston Abbey, there we unloaded and looked about for a place to picnic in. We vagued about until tea-time, and Mr. H. and Moritz dragged Viddy and I about in a cart, it was such fun. After tea we sang catches in the Abbey and played at Petit Pacquet in the field outside. Then we packed ourselves up and drove home.

There was to be a dinner-party that night, but the nausea that came over us at the thought of appearing in our whites was such that we wore our blacks, and I was very glad we did for of all the fiends I ever saw those eight people who came to dinner were the worst. Viddy and I and Helen always 'tead' (which we were very glad of) but today Lady Buxton said she thought I ought to dine, so I had been bemoaning myself, thinking that I should have to be portioned off to some excruciating parson, but to my great joy I found there was the usual enormous preponderance of females, so luckily for us Marie and I had to take each other in, and what a jolly dinner we had for Moritz was on the other side and no 'nips' (frumps) any-where near. After dinner we began to be awfully bored, for we had meant to play Rats and Ferrets, but we had to begin a stodgy game of Old Maid, just us two, Marie, Rachel and a Miss Joly. However, just as our spirits were sinking away altogether and soon after the gentlemen came in, Rachel told us Lady B. had said we might play all the same, so you can imagine we scurried off pretty quick, leaving all the oldies buried in spiders' nests (not their bodies but their minds). We were soon plunged into the midst of a most stunning game, but of course, my dear girl, we had hardly begun to get thoroughly into it when the door was opened and 'Prayers' bawled in – it was so tiresome. Then came the light, showing us all in the most splendid places – Mr. Hubbard standing bolt upright on the table and Marie sitting on the top of the Harmonium. As for me, to this day I don't know what I was sitting on, but it felt remarkably like best bonnets, and such I've no doubt it was. We had of course all to troop in (ten o'clock, you know) and there we found all the people and all the servants spudded about the room, it looked exactly like a Dissenting meeting.

After prayers all the frumps trooped off directly, which was delightful of them. Marie and I immediately cut out to a most stunning swing they have in the garden, and had a thorough good 'stander', going miles high to blow away the atmosphere of frumps. We were soon joined by Vi, Moritz, Kitty, Anna, Rachel, Mr. Hubbard and Miss Joly. We thought we must have some game, pitch dark and nearly eleven o'clock, so we were soon deep in a furious game of Witch. Oh, what a lark it was, we only played on a small part of the lawn, where there were lots of trees standing about, round which we dodged when we could make out the 'witch', and that was not often, for it was so dark the whole place seemed full of dark flitting forms – quite poetic – and when you did, you had to run for your life, which so winded everyone that they one by one retired towards the house without us seeing it – until, to our horror (because of Lady B.) Vi and I suddenly discovered we were playing quite alone with Moritz and Mr. Hubbard! So we simultaneously became rather tired and sauntered to the drawing-room window, where Marie

and some of the Buxtons were assembled. Mr. Hubbard then pro-
posed that we should all go for a walk to the Jetty, but no one dared
ask Lady B., so we had to go quietly off to bed.

Sculthorpe, August 29th, 1874

This day and October 2nd are the saddest anniversaries of the
whole year. Today, seven years ago, Mama died and on October
2nd it will be seven years since Papa died. How I do envy people
who have both their parents living – it is a great blessing for
which I am sure they are not sufficiently thankful. I think people
get to consider it as a matter of course that both their parents
should be alive and I don't think anyone who has not felt it can
realise what a blank they leave in one's life. I say that I envy
people who have both parents living, but by that I only mean the
fact, not the parents themselves, for I don't know a single woman
who I would have for a mother – or a man (except perhaps Uncle
Tum) who I would have for a father. Oh, I would not be anyone's
child but Papa's and Mama's.

From that text which says that a thousand years in Heaven are
as one night, I suppose it seems to Mama a very little time since
she died – but, oh, it does not seem so to me. I often long, with
an unutterable longing to see her again, just for one single minute
– not even to speak to – but just to look at her face again, for
alas, slowly but surely the memory of it is fading from my mind,
and now, if I shut my eyes and try to recall it, I can never, never
see it. . . . When I read over what I have written it sounds such
foolish, bookish humbug that I have half a mind to tear this page
out, for I can so well imagine, perhaps fifty years hence, when I
am either dead, or a very old woman, this day being laughed over
and set down in the hard way young people often judge, as
'Humbug' and 'Cant' etc. However, now it is written so here it
shall stay till, looking over the book, in a fit of disgust one day,
out it will come and perish by the flames.

September 2nd, 1874

The Ridsdales, Mr., Audrey, Cecy and Charlie came to

luncheon. They are a very eccentric family, Mr. R. being the parson of South Rainham. The girls had on red and white striped cotton underskirts with frills, and white piqué polonaises with red and white belts. They looked rather nice but evidently had on the most enormous amount of clean petticoats, which was very visible from their gowns sticking straight out as if they had on the most huge crinolines. Their stockings, capes and hats were awful, the former were white cotton and the latter black straw, very low and oval, trimmed with black velvet and the middle articles were perfectly colossal, made of black merino, trimmed with lace, like ours, only a good deal bigger, so you can imagine how they looked on them. However, their *tout ensemble* was infinitely better than the other day. Charlie wore a very nice little brown velveteen suit in which he looked very darling, and more like a robin than ever.

We had a very good luncheon indeed – a neck of mutton and fricasséed chicken with tongue – a plum tart, some pastry, stewed peaches and most delicious custard, besides two sorts of cake. When we had finished we took them round the garden and ate a little fruit. After several voyages in the punt we got a lot of peaches, plums, greengages, grapes etc. and had a feast. Then they had to go. I think they had enjoyed themselves very much. They are such fun and so original, they do amuse me so.

All the same it would be dreadful to have to keep them in order, they do such wild things that I defy anyone but a Ridsdale to think of. For instance, Charlie told me that the other day after we left he had been sent to bed early, so I asked him why. He had gone into the garden and met the gardener who, as Charlie said, 'had been having a drop too much beer with some of his friends – harvest time, you know. Sometimes a lot of them get down there together, and don't they kick up a jolly row.' Well, his story was that the gardener, being 'jolly drunk' had gone up to him and knocked him down on the path. Happily he was not hurt, though as Charlie said, 'he might have broke my neck', but as he didn't Charlie thought he would play him some trick, so he said, 'may I set fire to you?' and on the gardener saying 'yes', he actually

struck a fuse, of which he had a box in his pocket, and set fire
to his shirt sleeve! Which, being old and dry, burnt like anything,
happily although the man was drunk he had enough sense to put
it out but not until, as Charlie said, 'it had *stung him up well.*'
This was the reason why he had been sent to bed, and I'm sure I
don't wonder he was.

Runcton, September 3rd, 1874

Here we are, safe at home again. We arrived at Lynn about
eleven-thirty, and had the usual stuffy, rumbly drive in the
'Bathing Machine'. Oh, how well I know those coming homes –
I have arrived, as from Cromer with Vi, when there was no one
but Grobee to welcome one, which was very slow, and again we
have come home when there were a good many here – so it is not
that part one knows so well – it is the drive, the familiar objects
that keep appearing. First, when you get out of the train the
reigning 'John' (our men are always called John), then the bus
(alias Bathing Machine), then the Livery Stables, then the Gates,
then the Bridge (when we were twinks *Who stole the plums?* was
written in large red letters on one side wall – we always used to
look out for this, I never remember to have seen it really, though
I always pretended to for fear of being thought stupid), then
Mrs. Mason's house (which when we are going to a concert at
Lynn is always the point where I begin to put on my gloves),
then the two hills, after the last one you are getting very close
and in a minute you reach the fourteen acres, from there you can
see the turning and the Park.

Having passed the little plantation, with an elegant curve
Robert sweeps round the corner, and from there you catch your
first glimpse of the dear old house, two minutes more drive and
the carriage stops at the Approach Gates, by that time one's
excitement, which has been slowly working up all the way from
Lynn, has arrived at the highest pitch, and the bus seems to crawl
up the Approach, then the door is opened – pell mell everyone
jumps out – all the 'homeites' rush downstairs and the grand
finale takes place.

Sunday, October 4th, 1874

Uncle Tum and Aunt Kitty came to luncheon and chose all the pictures that are to go to the Art Loan, the exhibition which is to be held next week in Lynn for the benefit of the church. The Opie of Hudson Gurney, and the copy of the picture of Catherine Bell by Collins from the anteroom are going; the St. Francis by Rafaelo di Spagna, and the old Crome from the drawing-room, our Grandmama by Leslie, and a boy wild fowl shooting by King (from Grandpapa's sitting-room) are, I think, all. Those modern Dresden table dishes from the drawing-room are to go too, and *fancy*, Uncle Tum is actually going to exhibit *our painted tiles!* Isn't it jolly for us? Oh, that man is so delightful, I am sure others would not have thought of it.

October 6th, 1874

It was bitterly cold and windy, but poor old Grobee walked up and down, up and down the Approach for a whole hour, watching for Uncle Charles (Gurney) who was coming down for a few nights – he was so longing to see him. Uncle Charles arrived, he is so good-looking, at least 'de profile', and he is so nice and *mince* and tall. It is so delightful that he has got a wild rage for painting on china, he has brought all his paints down and says he will teach us and tell us all about it. After dinner I got out designs, transfer paper, tracing paper etc. and one of our old brick tiles – and Uncle Charles showed me how to draw on it with the prepared ink for painting, which was rather fun.

October 12th, 1874

The Exhibition opened today, we all went in at twelve. The Art Loan was formally opened by the Mayor and Corporation in all their robes, with Mace bearers and a lot of other humbugging old men. The Mayor made a speech and so did Uncle Tum. There were a good many people there, and really one could hardly look at the things for the first hour, one had to be constantly speaking to people. Our tiles really looked very well and nearly everyone we knew spoke to us about them and admired them so

93

much till one did not know what to say, it got quite tiresome. Of course *the* picture was the *Belisarius* from Raynham – I had often seen it before but never in such a good light. It really is a wonderful picture, you *couldn't* say it was beautiful or lovely, but it is wonderful. A picture one likes to look at but one wouldn't care the least to have.

Saturday, October 17th, 1874

There was great excitement among us this morning, for the Berties had settled to come over to Lynn for the day to see the Exhibition. We were quite wild about it, arranging what we were to wear etc. and it was for that that Amy had been working so hard at Limps' hat, to get it done in time. She put in a pale blue feather this morning for the finishing touch, and really it is an awfully pretty hat. We wore our new gowns for the first time, and oh – oh – oh, how hideous they are. In the first place the stuff is perfectly frightful. Amy lays all the blame on the *façon* but I know better. What *could* be more unbecoming, more hard, more iron, more ungraceful, more inartistic, more *servant-like* than dull grey-brown *linsey*? There is no stuff I think so detestable and it really was *horrid* of Amy to get it for us. She never asked me if I would like it, in fact she *never even told* me she was going to get it, but calmly came back from Lynn one day with an enormous bale of this horrible stuff. I said at once I never saw anything so hideous in my life. Don't you think it is very hard to have to wear these odious things *every day* for nearly six months, when we might have had nice soft lady-like homespun for much less money? She would never have bought such a thing for herself, and then, to make them 'nicer' still, Stanbrook has gone and made them more abominably than any other gowns she has ever made.

Oh, Amy is so tiresome about clothes, she has been dilly-dallying so about ordering our hats that they won't be ready for weeks, and *en attendant* Vi and I have nothing but our light summery wedding hats, trimmed with white feathers, to wear over our hatefuls and our thick winter jackets. Even Amy thought mine was too disreputable, so Clem lent me her black hat and I took out the white feather and put in a black one instead. I must say it suited me very well, much better than any hat I ever had. Oh, any nice clo' make one feel a different person, at least it does me, but perhaps that's because I am always such an old dowdy drudge.

Saturday, October 24th, 1874

After dinner we went off to the Art Loan again and had a very jolly evening there. First there was music, the band and dreader women singing, after that there was an auction of some wretched old water-colours – for the fund. Oh, how feeble they were, and no one would bid for them . . . after that there was some more music, several people made speeches, and then the exhibition closed and everyone had to leave the room – *God Save the Queen* sounding all over the place. The Exhibition was declared to have been a thorough success, for after paying all expenses (which amounted to £170), they had nearly £500 clear for the church. When everyone had left we, that is to say Uncle Tum, Uncle Charles, Clem, us three and Mort and Gee had a large supper of oysters, porter and thin bread and butter at the Refreshment Buffet, which I did not particularly care for as I can't endure either oysters or porter – so I had to content myself with the other thing – but it was rather fun too, and they all seemed to be enjoying the cold fishy lumps, Clem alone eating a dozen. When we got home we had a small supper, just us and Uncle Charles in the school-room, at which I made up for all deficiencies in Lynn.

October 28th, 1874

Aunt Bache had a few words with Clem about Vi and I being confirmed. I knew it would come this visit. Preparation, Confirmation, the Bishop, caps and all the rest of it, have been hanging, like an enormous cloud, over our poor heads for some time past, and now it has burst and is raining hard in the shape of lectures. We had our choice whether we should be confirmed with Eva this November, or at Sculthorpe, after being prepared by Uncle Herb, next July. At first we determined on the latter – because it was further off, but the more we thought of the long preparation by Uncle Herb, with Mary Jones for a fellow candidate, and a consequent long visit to Scully, the more awful it grew and we slowly, after well weighing both sides of the question, veered round and settled to be done at Lynn. Now that's far the worst part of it – the crowds and crowds – of horrible staring Linnets there will be everywhere, It quite makes me shudder to think of them, and they all know who we are – why it will be worse than being married, for there won't be the bridegroom to support one, and it is no good saying there are such a lot of them that one won't be noticed – I know better, everyone else is about four feet high and dressed in dark stuff, while we shall rise like two enormous pillars of salt out of the midst of them. Won't it be appalling? Now at all events at Scully we should not be so much known, all Fakenhamites would look at Mary and Katy – we should be mere nonentities.

But I almost incline to get it over as soon as possible and have done with it – like the powders one used to have in one's youth. Now this sounds very wicked and I dare say future generations will think what a heathen Laura Troubridge must have been, but they will be quite mistaken. It is not the religious part I am talking about at all. Of course that is very right and very solemn and I hope I shall feel all I ought, but it is the people I hate. Oh how I wish it was all over.

After luncheon we had to go down and tell Uncle Herb what we had decided, and he talked to us for three quarters of an hour without stopping. I thought he spoke very well indeed, I liked what he said, it was not pompous or prosy and it was to the point. It might have been rather shorter, but that one couldn't well expect.

October 29th, 1874

I am glad to say some new evening gowns were ordered for us in Lynn – dark blue – naval blue cashmere. I should think they would be rather nice and I'm sure it's a *comfort* to have *something* new, really we were *not* respectable in our black grenadines, mine is literally out at elbows and the whole thing is *en lambeaux,* and our whites are hardly better. Oh, I do hate being disreputable, and it is nonsense saying one doesn't see anyone down here so it does not matter, for it does, we often see people, and I'm sure I feel as if I was always dressing – besides one does like to be decent for oneself. I believe if I have worn that old black once I have worn it a hundred times.

October 30th, 1874

I had a delightful painting morning, all en famille in the sitting-room. I worked at a new sort of tile I am doing, from that funny old picture of Darnley in the dining-room. I liked doing it very much and did it rather well. Aunt Bache liked it so much that she is going to have her set all in that style, from pictures in the house. She said she wanted to give three shillings each for them instead of half-a-crown as she thought they were worth it. Of course we didn't raise any objection and really they are *much* more trouble than the others.

November 3rd, 1874

By way of something *entirely* new this morning, we first had lessons, then tennis and then Italian and painting till lunch. Isn't it wonderful how exactly alike our days are? It must be that that makes the time always pass so quickly. Time really seems to fly, why Christmas will be here in no time now, and it can't have been more than a week or two since last Christmas. Oh dear, how old we are all getting – fancy, I am now in my seventeenth year, isn't it sad? I shall soon be an 'oldy'. I shan't wear a cap, oh yes, I think I shall though, because they are rather becoming, but not an awful erection of blonde and artificial flowers, like one generally sees. I shan't always be talking of *lessons* or *mapping out everyone's time for them,* or going through whole pedigrees, like oldies generally do, ugh, they *are* so sodden. What a pity it is everyone can't always be young and nice.

November 13th, 1874

This was the day of the Ball [at Huntingdon, Amy's first ball]. A grand excitement, and our hopes had been high about the gown, but alas when the box arrived and we took it out each one's private verdict was, 'this gown is a failure!' Poor Amy's face, it grew longer and longer, and her eyebrows nearly met in the middle of her forehead. Oh, I was so sorry. However, the trial had still to be made and the gown to be tried on. Vi and I had to go down to the Rec. on a message from Grobee, but she promised not to take it off till we had seen it. And, no, I shall *never* forget what she looked like when we opened the door. It was a bitterly cold day and therefore her face, arms and neck were red, purple and pinched. Her face, no, I can't express the misery of it – she was very red and on the *verge* of crying, she really did cry when we talked it over and I really don't wonder. It *was* such a disappointment. Such a gown it was and such a figure she looked.

To begin at the bottom, the *coupe* of that skirt! She might almost have had a crinny on, it did everything it ought not to have, it stuck out at the sides and didn't trail behind, the glacé silk slip was so shiny it looked quite varnished, the puffings of the tulle 'over' were so skimpy and thin they did not soften it a bit, and instead of looking like a hazy white cloud it looked a simple glacé silk balloon. *Then*, the body – it had a *bertha* about large enough for Aunt Bache, trimmed with rows of enormous goffered tulle frills, each one *headed* with a white *cotton* braid – the effect was not sweet – another enormous frill went round the neck, making it a high low neck, always so ugly, and to complete it the sleeves consisted of a simple enormous bag of glacé silk, very nearly reaching the elbow and perfectly colossal, sticking our exactly like *doll's crinolines*. Add to this, untidy rumpled hair, a red, cryish *miserable* face, red arms – ditto neck and you will have some idea of how she looked. We almost laughed, it was so awful and so like the worldly woman in the *Sunday at Home*.

"Her Majesty in giving the medal to Sir Thomas Troubridge who had lost both his feet in action, leant over the chair of the maimed veteran and at the same time bestowed on him the honour of being her Aide de-Camp." — *May 18th, 1856.*

West front of The Hall, North Runcton, near King's Lynn, Norfolk before the gates were moved to face the long drive.
The home of Daniel Gurney who left his Quaker background at Earlham to set up his own family at Runcton and where the young
Troubridges were brought up after both parents died. Pencil, ink and wash drawing by a nineteen-year old artist called King (forename

Above *Tom, Ernest, Vi, Laura, Amy and Helen Troubridge (1882).*

Right *Life-size pastel portrait of Daniel Gurney painted from memory in 1901-02 by his granddaughter, Laura (Troubridge) Hope, over twenty years after his death. It was considered "a very good likeness".*

Below *Sir Thomas and Lady Troubridge (née Harriet Gurney), parents of the six children shown above. They died within five weeks of each other in 1867.*

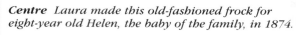

Top left *Amy at seventeen (1873) was really too old for the schoolroom life but lack of money ruled out any alternative.*

Centre *Laura made this old-fashioned frock for eight-year old Helen, the baby of the family, in 1874.*

Top right *Laura at fifteen (1873) moved easily between all ages and was more reconciled to their confined existence at Runcton.*

Above left *Eleven-year old Ernest photographed in his father's old hunting coat (1873).*

Above right *Ernest, seated, with his elder brother Tom, aged thirteen and fifteen, in their cadet uniforms (1875).*

Left *Laura, at nearly seventeen, with Ernest (still only twelve) acting as the necessary chaperon on their surreptitious expedition to the Burlington Arcade in 1875.*

Above Vi as an 18th-century vivandière with her little barrel of brandy, ready to minister to the French soldiers in times of war. Her costume, designed by Laura, was declared the best of the ladies at the Dunstan Fancy Ball, 1882.

Above right The beach at Cromer where Laura escaped to go sailing before joining the bathing machines with the official Buxton party in 1874.

Right Helen is at last growing up and is very popular among her Gurney uncles and aunts and their large families.

Far Right Amy, dressed for a walk along the seashore at Hunstanton with her collie Logie for company (1884).

Above left *Tom was gazetted in 1879 and joined his regiment, the 1st Battalion of the 60th Rifles, at Winchester. He was later stationed at Limerick from where he, with his sisters, spent their summer holiday at Knocklofty (1884).*

Above right *"Cressie" Cresswell was a fellow undergraduate of Oscar Wilde's at Oxford. When he gave a tea party for the great man in 1883, Laura found Wilde to b̶ "all monologue and not conversation".*

Below *Laura's view of herself talking to the peacock at Runcton, her childhood home, drawn when she was about twelve-years old.*

Above left Laura's pencil sketch of her favourite brother Ernest in 1883.

Above right It was Vi's tile design of a feckless youth "He must hunger in frost - that will not worke in heate" that inspired Oscar Wilde's sonnet "Wasted Days (From a picture painted by Miss V.T.)" in 1877. When it was pointed out that the sonnet would be more appropriately addressed to a female than a youth ("A fair slim boy not made for this worlde's pain ...") Wilde rewrote it as "Madonna Mia" for his collected poems (Bogue's edition, 1881).

Right Laura's self-sketch as "Jenny" in W.S. Gilbert's "Sweethearts" which she performed in front of the Prince and Princess of Wales (1884).

Above Laura *and her fiancé* Adrian Hope *in 1884, the year of their engagement. Little did they know that it would be exactly four years before they could afford t[...] get married.*

Below *"Little Thumb floats down the river on the lily leaf", one of Laura's sepia line illustrations for her first book, "Little Thumb, a fairy story by Hans Andersen[...] published by Mansell in 1883.*

Country Life and London Visits

Sculthorpe, January 13th, 1875

We left home this morning, Vi and I and Eva [Gurney] for a
few days visit to Scully. I did not like leaving home, I never do,
but still I liked the prospect of the dance. The news on our
arrival was that the Cranmers wanted us to get up some Tableaux
Vivants on Friday night. We were rather bored because they
have not thought of anything but have counted entirely upon
us and I do so hate organising things, as of course we shall have
to do.

We met Lawrence [Jones] riding, he was very nice but did not
look at all at his *avantage* as he was on a very small pony which
made him look so enormous, but Eva thought him much better
looking than she expected from his photograph. He has such a
nice face, dear boy.

Sitting in the West Room after tea we talked over all the pros
and cons of our toilettes for tomorrow night. It is the most
aggravating thing our yellow tarlatans not being finished, just
like our luck. At last we settled on our blue cashmeres with the
white fichus. Of course there would have been no discussion at
all if it had not been for the two evenings, which we had not
counted on, and the question was – could we wear the same gowns
twice, or would we be obliged to wear our hateful white muslins
at one, and if so at which should we be victimised? I think in a
case like that it is much better to please oneself, don't you? And
I know I should have been miserable in my white; why it is so
rotten that one pull would tear it all to pieces, and you know how
one gets knocked about at a children's party. After dinner, Aunt
Bache said she wanted to practise the figures of the Quadrilles,
so that, when she was asked tomorrow she might dance. It was
rather awkward, as we were only four, so we had to manage with

a chair for Aunt Bache's partner, Vi and I were her vis-à-vis, and Eva played the piano. Oh, how we laughed, we could hardly dance, to see her 'setting to' and 'turning' with this chair!

Thursday, January 14th, 1875

In trooped all the Cranmer children, and after a good deal of discussion we settled on four Tableaux, two scenes from *Beauty and the Beast* (after Walter Crane's illustrations); *William Tell shooting the Apple*, and a scene of Falstaff and the Fairies from *The Merry Wives of Windsor*. Lady Jones undertook the Beast's head, to be manufactured out of an old foot fur, so we only undertook the dressing of Beauty (Vi), and one of the sisters (Eva), the other sister (Kate) they had a gown for. Lawrence, of course, had to take *all* the principal men's parts.

We three went in to a very good tea, fried eggs and partridge, but before that we settled about the Tableaux dresses. Of course the mauve satin was far nicer than the red silk, particularly as it had a very pretty peaked body, so Eva and I drew lots for it and she got it, which was rather a bore. Of course these gowns were merely long trailing evening dresses and we had to attack them and transform them into the most elegant sort of Dolly Varden Pompadour costumes. Vi was the wretched victim or rather block; I pinned and tacked the mauve satin to be finished to-morrow. Then I attacked the red silk which I did on Eva and with very 'tweet' results, though of course it will never look as nice as the mauve satin. We went to dress for the *dance* at about six, though we were not to start till seven, but it is much nicer to have lots of time and to chat about it and dawdle and take things easy, particularly one's coiffure – which is ruination to do in a hurry.

We three and Bache went to Cranmer in their brougham, and a nice squash it was too. Our stuffy drive is over at last and the doors are thrown open. We find, when we have uncloaked, a good many people assembled in the inner hall, as tea has been going on in the dining-room ever since six. We however do not go in, the recollection of the fried eggs and partridge being too fresh in our minds. Soon everyone appears in the drawing-room and the dance commences with the well-known and much abused *First Quadrille*. I danced it with L. and we had rather fun because Vi and Tom were our vis-à-vis. There now, if I haven't entirely forgotten to say anything about the boys. They are both staying at Cranmer for the night on their way back from Hopton. We were awfully glad to see them and they were ditto. It always is so jolly to have a brother or two to fall back on if you haven't a partner. They were such darlings and both looked very nice. They both fell very much in love with Allie Seymour, a very pretty little girl who was there and kept begging her to dance with them.

I danced every dance except Sir Roger, at the end, which I sat out with Lawrence, and one Lancers. I had great fun at supper too with L. Altogether it was a much nicer party than usual, everyone seemed to dance with such spirit and all the children *could* dance, which was a great mercy, in fact some danced very well indeed – two little Colvin girls in particular, Amy and Polly (twins and exactly alike). They *did* look such darlings in black velvet frocks, short and plain, long black stockings, pale pink wide sashes, bows in their hair, short sleeves tied with pink ribbons and pink rosettes on their shoes.

The party broke up quite early, about twelve. That's the mistake of their parties, they begin so much too early – why we had five hours of it, and some came at six! Eva, who had made great friends with L. told me he wanted awfully to have the Tableau of *Taking the Veil* again, and said he hoped I would be the nun. He told Eva about his cutting off a piece of my hair years ago. Fancy his remembering it, though I don't see why he shouldn't as well as I – and I remember it perfectly. I can see him now, in his long red robes and tall gold mitre, bending over me. I can *feel* how I felt in that gown, a white one, high with a silver band – no ornaments, and a long, long train. I can feel his hand in my hair, and see his face laughing as he held up a long piece he had cut off, just as the curtain had dropped. I remember he would not let me have it, though I chased him and tried to tear it away! Oh, a long time ago – like a sort of dream, as all memories are.

Friday, January 15th, 1875

We were up very late, after breakfast we settled upstairs for a hard working morning on the Tableaux dresses. First we did Vi's petticoat, for we settled she as *Beauty* was to wear the mauve and yellow – I then made Vi's cap, cut the fichus, cut the frills and made Kate's cap. From three till six we were hard at work, I did get so sick of it! But we thoroughly finished everything by then and packed them all up too. I did both the gowns and was rather proud of them. Tea at six was very acceptable. Soon after I went up to dress. As I was to 'take the veil' I wore my old white muslin gown, with Vi's put on as a train. I had a chemisette to make my gown high, and no ornaments. Of course my toilette was very dreader but we had so much to do to the others there was no time to make me anything, and I forgot my *sloncherie* in looking at Vi, who did look so lovely.

We arrived at Cranmer at seven-thirty and were ushered upstairs to the green room, where we found all the girls and Mademoiselle Granier. L. was dressing for the first Tableau, in which he was to take the part of *Falstaff*. It was so ridiculous, we girls were all standing on the landing, he did not know we were there and suddenly appeared on the landing above and lent over the bannisters to call someone. I say he did, but really I could hardly believe it was him – a great horrible fat, black-bearded man – no more like L. than like me. Hideous he looked, really *hideous*, with his great bushy black beard and moustache and his scowling eyebrows above, very wicked. Oh, he must *never* grow a beard, I *shall never* speak to him if he does. He gave a loud shriek when he saw us and tore back to his room. Of course we all roared with laughter.

Mademoiselle Granier began to dress the *Fairies* and Eva and I helped. They really looked quite pretty, but their Tableau turned out to be – well – I thought not very pretty. There was no scenery *whatever*, merely a green baize curtain hung up behind them. It required such a *very* strong imagination to fancy them in a forest. Also the lights were so badly managed, or rather there were none at all except one large lamp, plainly visible in the middle of the floor. Also *Falstaff* was so *wretchedly* got up. He would have entirely spoilt it to my mind, however good the scenery and lights had been. Imagine a very fat (he was all stuffed with pillows), oldish, perfectly modern man out shooting and you will see him as he was. He had on grey shooting knicker-bockers, brown woollen stockings, a vague brown coat and a *very* small grey 'Wabbles' hat!

Then we all went up to dress for *Beauty and the Beast*. Oh, how pretty Vi looked, with her black hair combed right down over her forehead and fluffed out behind, her pale face under it looked exactly like some beautiful old miniature. Eva looked very well indeed in a bright red silk gown, Kate had on what was really far the best dress of the three – light blue and white brocade that had belonged to her great-grandmother. This Tableau was certainly better than the other, but there were the same mistakes as to light and scenery, and the grouping was not very good – also they all laughed. Poor L. was the father, and I don't wonder he laughed, for he told me afterwards he had on a pair of spectacles that magnified *double* – and so Vi, to whom he was present-ing the rose, seemed to be a sort of vague mauve and yellow cloud.

Next came *William Tell*, with Mary and Gerty as Swiss peas-ants, looking very well. L. I liked much as *Tell* in breeches and boots, a tight grey tunic, red sash, a large horn slung across his shoulders, and large black hat with a bunch of cock's feathers. Then came the last Tableau, *Taking the Veil*. I was the *Novice* (or whatever the victim is called), L. was the *Cardinal*, the two Lee Warners and Kate were *nuns* and Willoughby and Chandos L. W. were *acolytes*. (They looked darlings in white night-gowns and red sashes). I was not dressed up at all – my hair (my only beauty) was down, it was very much admired, which I was glad of. I really have got heaps and it is very long and soft, though no one would know I had above six hairs on my head from the way I do it. I was kneeling in front, at L's feet, he was bending down, with his large scissors and some of my hair in his hands. The three nuns stood behind, holding a large veil over my head and the acolytes stood on each side with lighted tapers in their hands. I was perfectly still and told the beads of my long black rosary with becoming solemnity, but the wretched little boys giggled and quite spoilt the effect. I made L. promise, before he touched my hair, he would not cut any off – for he looked so wicked when he asked me if I remembered it last time that I thought the precaution rather necessary.

I enjoyed myself after the Tableaux *very* much and had *some* really nice dances. I made great friends with Alice Lee Warner. I was galloping with Sir Willoughbub and she with old Mr. Donel at the same time, and we both agreed it was detestable to dance with old men.

Back at Runcton, January 18th, 1875

Vi and I felt so longing to spend some of our Uncle Herb tip money – it already burned our pockets, so we settled to have a grand 'Lynning' and make large investments in old china – our present rage. We three (Amy came too), with Tom as protector, set off directly after lunch, wrapped in our scarlet blanket Invernesses (perfectly brand new). At Goldings Vi bought a very handsome large Mason Ironstone plate for two shillings. It will look very well in our room. Amy bought a nice blue and white plate (we think Nankin). We went on to Nurse, the watch-maker's (he is also a china dealer), he really had some very nice things and not at all expensive either. Amy and Tom both invested in Delft plates and I bought a delicious tall blue and white vase for two shillings. Then we went to Plowright's and there I bought a most fascinating sort of large blue and white pot. I loved it and think it will have a very good effect planted with yellow crocuses in our room.

Then we walked all about Lynn and made voyages of dis-covery down unknown back streets, but they generally smelt so that we had to turn back. We had the china fever very hot upon us, and even a drizzly downpour and only two umbrellas between us did not damp our ardour.

One day soon after this we were wondering where Tom was, and Amy said, 'I am sure that boy has taken the opportunity while we were out to dash off to the Alms-houses and secure all the old china.' We all said we did not think he would do anything so nasty, but she was quite right. We thought that very likely some of the old people in the village might have some china they would like to sell us, so we settled to make a china-hunting expedition. When Tom – with Ernest – reappeared Amy called out, 'where have you been?' Tom bawled out – 'we went rabbiting.' Amy said, 'have you been to the Alms-houses?' They only answered by very guilty laughter. Tom's defence was rather vague – he said they hadn't meant to go when they first went out, but as they were passing the Alms-houses they thought they might as well go in, but afterwards it turned out they had been nearly round the village. However their spoils did not amount to much, except for a very pretty rosebud pattern sugar basin marked 'A.W.' – I suppose Worcester.

We grew more amicable over our luncheon and settled to have a thorough afternoon of it and go all over the place. We went first to Ann Trower, for the boys said she had a good deal more of the Worcester rosebud tea service that she would not mind 'parting with'. Oh, that 'parting with' – how sick we got of it by the end of the day. We used it on every occasion, for instance when we knocked anywhere and the door opened we always began with, 'We are making a collection of old china things and wondered if you have any you wouldn't mind parting with.' Then, when they showed us things it was, 'Well, would you mind parting with this?' then if they demurred we always said, 'of course if you would rather not part with this we would not think of taking it,' or 'are you quite sure you don't mind parting with this?' etc. etc. We had great success at Ann Trower's; she actually brought out six cups and saucers and a china tea-pot, all of that same rosebud set, and absolutely *refused* to take anything for the service except photographs of us all.

Our next visit was to Ann Story's, where Clem and Amy came out triumphantly carrying two pretty old Lowestoft bowls, one was very much cracked and the other whole, except for one piece which she had. Altogether they were undoubtedly the best things we had found yet. We soon arrived at the Alms-houses, first we went to the Donaldson's, they opened their cupboard and we fished out several things – a blue Spode plate, for which we gave a shilling, another plate, a vague jug and a bowl, very coarsely painted and marked with an anchor, this we thought at first was Chelsea, but know since that it is Davenport. We gave them half-a-crown for the lot and they were so pleased.

Mrs. Adams we visited next. She had the rheumatics and seemed rather a cross old thing – perhaps in consequence, however it was her china we wanted and not her, so that did not matter much. She had six plates, old Delft, with a border of raised flowers round them and a funny little picture of 'Queen Victoria afore she came to the throne'. We gave her three shillings for these and three more for some other things. We borrowed a large washing basket to carry our spoils in, and Vi, Ernest and Limps set off home with it. Amy, Clem, Tom and I went on to Robert Harris. There we reaped up a tea-pot, for which we gave a shilling. (The next morning he sent up two nice cups and saucers to match as a present.) We did a lot more visits in the afternoon, but it began to drizzle so we went home.

After tea was over we divided all the spoils into six equal lots; we had six tea-pots, so we had one each. Of course some were not so nice as others but we made the other things counterbalance that. We were a long time doing it, and I must say we did it very well indeed – nothing could have been fairer, and the proof of this was that when we drew lots no one would exchange a single thing. I was very pleased with mine. Our accounts were in a *hopeless* state of confusion for we had taken no notes of what we paid or who paid it and no one seemed to know how much they had when they started, so everyone's money was mixed up in the most tiresome way. We were more than an hour getting it all right. At last we made out we had spent altogether eighteen shillings – so this, divided into six equal parts of three shillings is all we each had to pay. Then the difficulty was to know who was to pay who, and long, long discussions followed. I was glad to say I was entirely out of them for as I had only fourpence in my pocket when I started no one owed me anything.

After supper Vi and I and Ernest went to our room and covered a long box with red baize. We are going to fix it on the wall, with china inside and on the top. We had rather fun over it.

Friday, January 22nd, 1875

After luncheon we three and Clem started in the pony carriage to go round West Winch, china-hunting. We were very unsuccessful all the first part but were rewarded by treasures at the end. On the way home our good genius prompted us to stop at two cottages together. We said we would try there as a last forlorn hope, but Amy flatly refused to get out for she said she had had so many *rebuffades* that she was quite sick of them, and Clem said she felt so tired she could not come, so Vi and I had to venture in alone. When we came to the first of the two Vi said, 'don't let's go in here, there are no ornaments on the mantelpiece.'

So we passed to the next and one look through the window revived our sinking spirits, for there on the chimney-piece were five lovely blue and white cups and saucers. The door was opened by a man whose face I knew, he brought down the china directly, and some more of the same set from a cupboard and seemed delighted to sell it. We asked him his name, as there was a large picture of Grandpapa and one of Runcton on the wall, and he turned out to be Lincoln, the old butler who was discharged for drunkenness. Uncle Tum and Grandpapa allow him a pension – I believe he still drinks dreadfully – however he certainly was not drunk then, and did not look the least drinkish or horrible. He said there had been many more cups and saucers, and for all those he had given ten shillings. Of course the price was absurd – you certainly could not get one of those cups and saucers in Lynn for less than three or four shillings each, they are lovely old

blue Salopian with gold edges, handle-less and quite perfect.
However we did not tell him that. We bought four cups and
saucers for a shilling each and the two large saucers for a shilling
each too, which you see was a good deal more than what he said
he gave for them. He evidently did not know in the least who
we were, and he was awfully pleased with his six shillings.

Inspired with fresh hopes we went next door, but they had
nothing, the woman there asked if we were Miss Gurneys. We
told her who we were and she must have told Lincoln, for a day
or two after he came up bringing two more cups and saucers. He
gave them to Guddy for us, saying he hoped we would accept
them and that if he had known who we were he would not have
taken anything for the others. That was the grandest find either
of today, or yesterday, and put us all in a good humour.

Next day we went to Mrs. Secker's, and she presented us with
the most *splendid* old pottery figure I ever saw. It is a man and
woman walking arm in arm, both with waists just under their
arms, and the most killing hats. She absolutely refused to take
anything for it, though we tried to make her. She wanted to make
us a present of it and money, she said, would spoil the gift. She
kept saying, 'if yew *will* accept it yew're as *welcome* as a Prince –
after all your koindness to the choild and all – yew're roight
welcome to her.' Of course we thanked her tremendously. It is
awfully old, as she is over eighty and she told us it belonged to
her *husband's father's grandmother*! We drew lots for it, and woe
of woes, Amy got it – we others nearly howled with rage. We
also went to Mary Ling's – fancy, she told us she had had a good
many funny old saucers and things but as they were no use to
her and she did not want to leave rubbish to trouble people after
her death – she broke them up with a hammer and put them on
the road. Wasn't it idiotic of her? She said she was so sorry as
she would have liked to give them to us.

March, 1875 – A long ago memory
When my Mama died I felt everything was a sort of awful
blank. I remember how hard it seemed the sun should shine as

brightly as ever and people should sing and be merry outside when I was so unutterably miserable, for though a child's sorrow does not last like older people's, while it does it is very, very bitter. That such a thing as her death was possible, I had never even thought of – I never for one moment realised she was so ill as that. I remember it as if it was yesterday. Some niggers were singing and playing on the beach [at Yarmouth], Vi and I were with the crowd, laughing and looking on. Amy and Clem were sitting together a little way off, she was older and understood more about Mama. It was a glorious day, very hot, with the sun shining so brightly and the sea very calm. I was talking to a little friend who was standing with us, and said, 'my Mama is very ill in London now, but she is coming here when she gets better.' Just as I said that, I turned round and saw a woman come out of our house – which was just opposite, run across the street and put a fluttering yellow paper into Clem's hand. I saw she was crying and wondered vaguely what was the matter. The nigger began another song, I went on watching him. A minute after I heard my name called, Vi came and said, 'Clem says we must go in, and Amy is crying – has she been naughty?' I said, 'but why should we go in?' 'I don't know,' said Vi, 'but Clem said so.' So we two lagged crossly in after the others, I picked up Amy's pail on my way and dragged it after me by its long string. I tried to give it to her, but she was crying so she did not see – I wondered what she had done, but did not think much of it. Up we went across the road and into our house, a corner one with two stone lions on either side of the door, and the name *Britannia House* in large letters over the gate.

Up we went and took off our hats and jackets. Vi went down before me, and Amy too. I went slowly downstairs to the sitting-room, fastening my pinafore. I opened the door and looked round rather surprised, Amy and Vi were both crying, sitting near the window. Green Venetian blinds were down and the sun was shining brightly through the strips of wood. 'Vi,' I said, 'what are you crying for? Let's go and play with our dolls.' Then I stopped, for Clem came up to me and put her hand on my shoulder. I looked up in her face, astonished, for she was crying too. Never, if I live to be a hundred, shall I forget the awful feeling that came over me when I heard these words – 'your Mama is dead – ' I went and lay on the floor, with my head on a funny green sofa there was there, and cried as I have never cried since, and never had before. I tried to think it was not true, to fight against it, but the words kept ringing in my ears, 'Mama is dead – Mama is dead – you will never see her more – never more – never more.' I shall never forget that time, all the happiness seemed gone from our lives. Life had entirely changed for us, yet the nigger had not finished his songs and the sun was shining as brightly as ever.

When we had cried ourselves tired we talked a little about it. It made me so miserable to think I could never, never tell her many things I wanted ... I remember nothing more of that unhappy day, nor of the ones that followed. That morning only is engraved in my memory. What a sad, dull coming home it was a few days after that. No one to welcome us, poor Papa was still very weak and ill. He could only see three of us at a time; we went into the library, we three very quietly and kissed him as he lay in his armchair. How ill he looked, he hardly spoke above a whisper, we were almost frightened of him. Poor children, what a sad home it was for us, how we missed her everywhere. I used to wander about her room looking for traces of her. It seemed like some awful dream. I used to feel as if I had never really had Mama, so entirely was she gone.

We had not used the drawing-room since she died. One day I stole in on tiptoe across the room to the table, took up a book and began to look at it. Suddenly I turned round, the empty dreariness of the room frightened me – I fled like a thief, back to the warm nursery with the children playing about. The mood is gone – I cannot write a word more.

The end of April, 1875

We have had a rage for *spells* lately – old ones we find in books. This is one, to be done by four girls – Amy and I, Vi and Eva.

We wrote four gentlemen's names in full on separate slips of paper, and on a fifth the word *Death* must be written. These must all be folded, shuffled, and each must draw one. If all the girls draw gentlemen's names and leave *Death*, then the name they have each of them drawn will be that of their future husbands, but if one of them draws *Death* then none of the girls will marry any of the gentlemen whose names were written, and four more names must be written and drawn again. Well, we four did it. We all left *Death* – Amy drew *Lord Hastings* (she blushed), Eva *Mr. Bob Hodgson*, Vi *Edward Roger Murray Pratt*. This is the name I drew – *Lawrence Jones*. Then from vagueness, we thought we would all draw again, with the same names, to try if we should all get them again. We all left *Death* for the second time, but Vi had *Lord H.*, Eva *Mr. H.* and Amy *Mr. P.* This is the name I drew – *Lawrence*.

One evening in May, 1875

Amy and I are sitting in the drawing-room with Grandpapa. He has begun snoring again. How I *hate* snoring. I hope my husband (if I ever have one) won't snore, I really could not bear it. I shall have to ask beforehand. This will be the sort of thing – Impassioned lover, kneeling:

> 'Laura – Oh, dearest Laura, let me ask you to say one word –
> I love you – worship you – adore you – say – Oh, *will you*
> be my wife?'
> Laura, eagerly, with a searching glance – 'Do you snore?'
> Impassioned lover, mournfully – "Yes – '
> Laura, sternly, 'Then, no!' Lover falls back in a fit.
> Exit Laura – Tableau – Curtain falls . . .

Really, what nonsense I have been writing. I suppose it is the reaction after staid conversation with Grandpapa for an hour at dinner tonight. Yes, our dinner always lasts *an hour*. Imagine the waste of time, we have about three things to eat, and could do it all slowly in a quarter of an hour, but all the rest of the time is taken up, first with waiting between the courses for Grandpapa

to finish his food, and then, the worst time of all, after everything
has been taken away and dessert is on the table, Grandpapa turns
his chair round to the fire and remains there for nearly half an
hour while we have to wait round the table doing *nothing*, for
we rarely care for any dessert – not in winter – waiting and waiting, watching his back and getting so *intolerably* bored, till, at
last he comes to the table and eats a *very* large dessert, very,
very slowly.

Of course we always talk to him, we think of all sorts of things
to say that interest him, and are as nice to him as we can be, but
our 'asides' are odd and betray the state of our minds. Oh, what
joy when he makes the sign – we do not linger long I can tell you.
The sign is dipping his finger in his finger glass and touching his
lips with it, which he always does when he wants us to go. It is so
funny, because he hardly ever touches the water, so it is only a
form of dismissal.

Prayers will be announced in a minute. Heigh-ho, oh lack –
such is life. I hope they won't be very long, I don't think people
ought to have prayers on Sunday evening. One can't be fresh to
pray and pay attention after two long services. I know I am always
nearly asleep, for they last about half an hour and are generally
sermons or long religious letters from old books in the library.
They are often quite inappropriate. One he sometimes reads is
'addressed to men of high and influential position', which considering the audience consists of us girls and the maids is not very
well chosen.

What an odd time it was while the others were away. How
dull Amy and I used to get, we hardly ever laughed, never made
jokes or did absurd things. I assure you I felt quite old sometimes,
in the evenings, but of course that was all because of Grandpapa.
How can an old man of eighty-four, however delightful he may
be, and girls of sixteen and eighteen get on well together? He's
delightful for a short time, but oh so depressing for long – and
John Evelyn – John Evelyn – you odious man. After having read
out loud to Grandpapa four volumes, and the *Supplement* of his
book *The Records of the House of Gurney*, we have begun *John*

Evelyn's Diary – two very fat quarto volumes, and such a book!
Long, dull, prosy descriptions of churches and gardens, palaces,
scenery in Italy, France etc. or else – but I don't think I shall tell
you what the other parts are. But it is very awkward sometimes in
the middle of a sentence, or description, to stop short, stammer,
leave off and go on in quite another place, but it is no good. Old
books always are improper. People were coarse then and therefore what they wrote was too. Horrid people, and certainly that
is not a fit book for us to read, and Grandpapa ought to know it.
It would really be dreadful if anyone was there. Happily G. gets
so sleepy that it does not matter making it no sense.

This is how we spend our days: we are generally down by
eight, an hour of painting before prayers, ten minutes after
prayers (while he goes for his walk down the Long Walk and
back) I play valses and Amy valses – round and round – all about
the room, breakfast from nine-thirty till ten, lunch (with him) at
one-thirty, tea (tête-à-tête) at five – painting – lawn tennis –
painting – lawn tennis – all day long, varied with writing letters,
going down to Vall. or in the village. Six-thirty dinner till seven-
thirty, repression and unnecessary food. Heigh-ho, such is
life – peaches and joy – roaming the garden and fields from seven-
thirty till eight-thirty. Sodden, dull, hot times from eight-thirty
to nine-thirty or ten – a large fire, all the windows shut, a lamp
and three candles – on a lovely breathless evening, when we are
pining to be out and free – an hour and a half of this detestable
book, having to be nice and kind to him, talking – bawling into
his ears – oh, how cross we used to get [while the others were
away] – no wonder we feel old. Though, poor old thing, of
course one would not mind reading to him (now his eyes are
bad) if it only wasn't in our evenings that used to be so lovely.
And that fire – oh dear, a sickening stuffy heat, that makes one
feel quite spiritless and languid, with the birds singing outside,
the calm evening sky above and the soft evening air – all seeming
to call one out. At ten we were released and then we had rather
good times, not fun, we had got too dull for that. Amy used to
come to my room and there we installed ourselves till twelve or

past, chatting, reading, writing letters – or journals – and munching biscuits. And then, when we were sleepy off we used to go to bed, and that was the end of our days. How we longed for the others – there was a sort of unsatisfied incompleteness about the house – but now they're home again – Hooray.

A day at Boston, May 12th, 1875

Called at five-thirty – very sleepy and I don't wonder. Ugh, how I did hate getting up, the morning was dull and grey and I had not been to sleep till nearly twelve the night before. However I managed to lug myself up, as our train was to start at seven-thirty. Our party consisted of us two, Amy and myself, Uncle Tum, Aunt Kitty and Birdie Brett (who is staying at Vall.), and the object of our expedition was to see Boston Stump, which is a most beautiful old church, and any other interesting objects that might turn up.

To Vall. at six-thirty found them just ready to start. Uncle Tum was very amusing, though yawning, as indeed we all were. We arrived at Lynn in very good time, and got a carriage all to ourselves. Our journey was all through marsh land, how wonderfully flat Norfolk is, miles and miles one can see of green, green fields, with here and there a few poplars or sheep. Uncle Tum says they call the country about here 'New Holland'. At Spalding we changed and had a sort of breakfast of cups of tea and large, dry biscuits. I knew by that time we should have a jolly day, for everyone was in such jolly minds, there was not one cross, or even dull person the whole time.

As we got near Boston we all looked out for the Stump, which we soon espied, towering above everything else. The steeple is an immense height and the lantern is all open, altogether it is very fine (how like Grandpapa). When we got out of the station we made our way through the most funny little crooked, smelly back streets towards the Stump. The church is built quite on the edge of a small river, the tide was down and it all looked very muddy. We crossed a good iron bridge and got into quite a different part of the town with large streets and a great many shops. We came out into a market place, just under the church square and surrounded with houses, *exactly* like a foreign town. A grand market was going on and it all looked *so picturesque,* great stalls of oranges, cabbages and things, grey tent covers and lots of country people buying and selling. We were all enchanted with it, it was so different from the Lynn market, with nothing but a few old fish. Here there were all sorts of things, more like the Lynn Mart, only with no shows and a great many more booths with toys, gingerbreads, sweets, beads, stuffs, hats, sun-bonnets, knife-grinders, tinsmiths, old iron stalls, second-hand book stalls, a Nottingham lace stall, a rag stall, many crockery stalls, shoe-makers, old clothes buyers – and many others. We were so long looking about that the Stump was quite forgotten! We saw some very jolly shoe buckles and could not resist tearing in to buy them. That completed the illusion of a foreign town, for the people all spoke French.

After buying two pairs of buckles (they were sixpence apiece and very pretty, made of German silver) we dashed after Uncle Tum and Aunt Kitty who were in the church. It is really glorious, an enormous building, wider than any Cathedral in England, with one exception. The height is wonderful, I do not know anything about architecture, but I believe it was mostly built in the fifteenth century. There were two good coloured windows and two very inferior ones, and a great deal of lovely carving.

We went back to the buckle shop, then we found a lace stall, all Nottingham lace, very pretty and too absurdly cheap – about a quarter of a yard wide for twopence. We bought heaps of it, of all sorts and sizes, for furniture you know. Then we explored and came to a shoemaker's with lots of holland shoes. Amy bought a pair for lawn tennis, laced with red for three shillings. We asked the man if there was anything particular going on in the town, and he told us of an Art Loan Exhibition to which we immediately went and spent about two hours. There was a delicious old Majolica plate, from the South Kensington Museum, which we quickly sketched.

Then we went back to the market with a band playing hand

bells – a little girl drummer, dressed as a *Vivandiere*. It was a delightful day, but the longest day must end. Amen.

June 2nd, 1875

Time ten-thirty p.m., and where do you think I am? Why lying full length across a very comfortable bed in a spare bedroom at Abbey Lodge, Hanover Gate, London! There, what do you think of that?

Well, we arrived here [to stay with the de Bunsens] four o'clock on Tuesday, June 2nd, dirty – dusty – hot and tired. Oh, that journey up. I had on shoes that were perfect *agony* – brand new, stiff like iron, tight and burning hot. I don't think I ever had such pain, I could have cried. They did not leave off for one single moment all those four hours. Of course I would have wrenched them off, only the carriage was full – *also* I was so dreadfully afraid I should not be able to get them on again, so I had to grin and bear it. We found Marie [de Bunsen] dressed ready to go out to tea – nice, wasn't it? She dined out, too, and Moritz and Monsieur. Of course they all apologised, hoped we would not be dull etc., but it really was rather rude, only I suppose they have so many people here that if they stayed in for them they would never go out at all. So Uncle Herb, who was staying the night, and we two sat down to dinner. After dinner we sat in the garden and had a long theological talk with Herb – it was interesting and he really was nice. He always is much better when Bache isn't there (often the case with married men). But wasn't it odd and unforeseen for our first night in London? A list of my clothes:

A Workhouse sheeting jacket, body and *tablier* – very long, to wear with dark blue frilled petticoat and sleeves – also ditto red. My last summer's grey, turned and refurbished. My old peacock cashmere evening, transformed into a day gown with long sleeves and a front piece of the same. A white piqué (originally Confirmation), trimmed with frills and *bouillonées* of white lawn – and that's all day gowns. For the evening, a black tarlatan, high, long sleeves, white fichu and a train (my first), also rather a pretty white muslin, with a nice little train, square and elbow sleeves, plissées with lace etc., and my dreadful yellow that I don't see myself wearing at all.

Then I have a very nice plain, thin, cloth tight jacket, dull black, rather long, with silk collar, fronts and cuffs – I like it. I have only one hat as yet, but am going to get another, the one I have is very coarse white straw, round, very wide brim, large, high crown, and trimmed with black ribbon and poppies.

June 3rd, 1875

One of the dullest days I ever spent. We did not go out the whole morning, Marie never even asked us if we would like to and we could not go on our own hook because Stanbrook [their maid] had not yet arrived. At about a quarter to four we set off, Madame, Amy, Moritz, Marie and I for a round of calls in the large open carriage, such a dull party. First we went to a Mrs. Derby Griffiths where there was to be a French recitation and some music. Here Madame said she could not take more than two, so I waited in the carriage, alone, for an hour – with rather a headache (from my hat which was very heavy), a dull book, a quiet street and a burning sun. It seemed so funny to be driving about London in a nice carriage again. I tried to think we were living as we were – and that I was waiting for Amy and Mama. Oh, how I wished it true. At last the realities came out. Then we went to Mrs. Willie something. Here I got out, but we did not stay more than ten minutes. I was so glad for I did not know a soul, however I had a brown bread ice, which was one tiny drop of consolation.

When we got back we found the Harfords had arrived (they are first cousins of Marie's). We hated their coming for we were afraid they would pair off with M. and that we should be more left in the lurch than ever, but really it turned out just the contrary. They are so nice to us and don't care very much for Marie – I mean they see her faults. We did not know this then and felt as though we should never laugh again. But we were quite wrong, for we had a delightful evening. Poppy Herbert came and we girls sat out till about eleven, laughing like anything – so much for the dumps.

Monday, June 7th, 1875

Met the Harfords by chance at the Baker Street Bazaar. Went a long walk with them. After luncheon, left to our own devices again – went to see Marie Vleminck [Clem's sister, who was governess to the Duke of Atholl's children]. She had to take the twinks [children] to a dancing class, we stayed as late as we could and then set out for home, walking. Oh, it was so jolly, we walked up to Hyde Park Corner and then all down Piccadilly. It was *crowded* – and rather improper – but after all, as we say, it's Madame de Bunsen's fault. She should look after us. If she does not give us any fun, why of course we must have some on our own hook, and then of course, *nobody* knows us.

We had such a stroke of luck here. We have been hunting high and low for some hats – well, Constance Harford told us of a shop in White Horse Street, but nobody could tell us where W.H.St. was – so we thought it rather hopeless, when, happening to look up on our way down Piccadilly, what should we see but White Horse Street staring us in the face. Wasn't it odd? Of course we went down it directly, such a funny little crooked street – a sort of mews, with no shops on one side and one or two dirty-looking ones on the other, but that exactly corresponded with the Harford description. Still, it did look too vague, we hunted high and low but could not see a ghost of a hat shop (rather a nice idea), and then came the second stroke of luck. We were standing at the corner of the street and Amy said, 'well, *I* don't see *any* hats,' and a man who was standing behind us said very politely, 'are you looking for the hat shop, Miss? It is the third door on the right.' And so we found it was, though we might have hunted for it till Doomsday, for there was not a sign of any hats. We found one quite the right shape only in brown, so we ordered two to be made in white, and they are to come to-morrow. Price: nine shillings and sixpence each untrimmed, which is rather pocket-draining.

They all dined out somewhere – it really is too shameful never taking Amy anywhere after all Madame de B. said when she was at Runcton. However, we had an awfully jolly evening, all because of the Harfords – talking, laughing, singing and playing the piano. Another evening we had great fun as Edmund and Charlie Leatham and Arthur Herbert dined and we went mad in the garden, playing games – witch, hide-and-seek in the dark, and danced Country Dances with no music on the grass – we were out till nearly eleven. Then we went up to the Harford's room (that is to say Amy and I, for poor Marie was driven off directly to bed by the relentless Cob – her maid), and there we hatched the most lovely plot – of course it is a dead secret. The ingredients are: all the de Bunsens dining out, four girls left alone at home – four gentlemen drop in (quite unexpectedly of course) *and* a hurdy-gurdy man (very odd), a nice smooth lawn – and eight willing pairs of feet tell the rest of the story. Won't it be a lark? That's all!

Tuesday, June 8th, 1875
Alas! Alas! Our lovely plot is entirely spoilt, for Marie stays at home tonight. Such a sell, I knew something tiresome would happen.

June 9th, 1875
A dull day. We wanted something to cheer us up dreadfully, therefore of course we had it. After leaving the Herberts we walked down Great Stanhope Street when who should we see but Sommy [Gurney]. We *were* so glad to see him as it happened he had nothing on hand, so he took us back to No. 27 Grosvenor Square, where they are staying with the Edward Scotts, to see Aunt Kitty, and afterwards walked back to Abbey Lodge with us, treating us to ices on the way. Something else happened too, for on the first day we were in London we passed a

delicious old curiosity shop in York Place and in the window was a most beautiful tea-set of old blue Lowestoft. We said directly that if Sommy came we would take him to see it, and so we did. Of course he went in and bought it directly. Such a bargain never was made, it is the finest old Lowestoft, with a blue border and gold monogram of W.B. and arms in the middle of each piece. There are thirty pieces and all quite perfect, and how much do you think he got it for? Five pounds!

Friday, June 11th, 1875
Booba [Aunt Bache's maid] came to escort us home in a cab – home, at least to a vague hotel – Storeys, No. 8 Dover Street, where we are going to stay a week with Bache and Herb. I think it will be very jolly.

Saturday, June 12th, 1875
An invitation came from the Willoughby Jones' saying that they had *one* spare stall for the morning performance of *Hamlet* with *Irving*. They said they would take one of us – of course Bache settled directly it was to be Amy, though Uncle Jimmy, who had just dropped in, wanted us to toss up and Amy herself wanted us to draw lots, but I gave up directly with a very good grace, considering that I would have given my eyes to go.

At about three, Bache and I and Billy [William Skipper, the man-servant], on the box, set off in a cab for our campaign – we drove to Soho Square and found the dear print shop, and there we stayed ages. Old Smith was such a dear old man, knew about everything, remembered Miss Troubridge perfectly and instantly brought forward several portfolios full of prints for us to look at. He had two of our great-grandfather that of course I bought directly. After that we routed about for more print shops, but were not very successful, so we went home, and I sat on the balcony till they came. They all said it (*Hamlet*) was too wonderful and splendid and that they had enjoyed it immensely. I told them they all looked as if they had been crying.

Sunday, June 13th, 1875

In the afternoon we went to Westminster Abbey. Uncle Herb knows Dean Stanley, so we went through his house and got into his pew, which was very lucky for us. It was the best place in the Abbey, and many people had to stand the whole time. The anthem was perfectly glorious, from Mozart's 12th Mass, which we know. We had to walk back in the rain as there were no cabs. Sir Willoughby and Lawrence caught us up, and L. escorted us to the Cochranes, where we were to have tea. I have discovered one thing in L. that I did not know before – he is very fond of pictures. We went wild over Ruskin's pamphlets, we discussed the Academy together, he is going for the second time to see it at eight o'clock tomorrow morning, and asked me to come with him – safe, you know!

The Cochranes were very nice, they had pretty gowns of dark olive green cashmere and silk; it suited Minnie very well. I never saw any people so interested as they are about our life and doings at Runcton. It is very easy to talk well and be amusing to people who are so interested as that. We told them about our plans for the future – our little house, the artistic home etc. They were very much amused, and we chaffed each other about our futures. We are to look out for a poor curate in Norfolk for Minnie, and she is going to look out for my very rich old man – Amy is to have a penniless bad artist, jolly for her. Dinner quietly, and went to bed early – what a wonder!

June 14th, 1875

At the National Gallery . . . perfectly absorbed in the pictures, we met E. R. Murray Pratt and one of his sisters. They both said they far preferred the Academy! Grovellers! Most exquisite pre-Raph. ones – hundreds of years old – by heavenly old Italian Masters. We went to the Howards in the evening. Lady Audrey was delightful as usual, Lady Booba was so nice and kind, but it was rather dreadful for me coming to be seen and all that sort of thing; however she is a very putting-at-ease person. (She is my Godmother, you know). Sir Hereward and Lady Wake (née

St. Aubyn) were there, he a funny little man, talked like a book in 'I', if you know what I mean. He drew well, there was a book of his there – clever I thought and amusing. He paints on china too, and gave us some useful hints.

Tuesday, June 15th, 1875

Amy and I went off in a cab with Herb to the South Kensington Museum. We saw some lovely things, I should think it would take two or three weeks to see it all properly. The pictures are nothing, but the china, antiquities, curiosities etc., are beautiful. We tore back to Dover Street to meet Ernest, who was to lunch with us on his way to Greenwich for the entrance exam to the Navy – oh, how I hope he will pass. Everyone says – Mr. Allen [the school master] and all – that he is sure to.

June 16th, 1875

We walked in the Park and met Uncle Charles. We told him we wanted so much to go to Princes, and asked him if he could possibly take us, and he said he would that afternoon. We got there by six – it was *perfectly crowded*. Uncle Charles said he had hardly ever seen it so full. There was a grand cricket match going on, but we did not care for that – the skating was what we loved. Oh, it looked perfectly *heavenly*, everyone gliding and flying about. I *longed* to do it, but no one may who is not a member. All the people were very well got up, some really beautiful dresses. We saw no falls, though there were lots of quite little girls skating. There is a large covered place with open arches all round, to skate in when it rains.

June 19th, 1875

Alas, our last day in dear, dear London. *What* fun we have had, how I wish we were going to stay longer. I do *love* London, it's such *fun*, one is always doing something heavenly. This morning we two and Ernest tore off quite surreptitiously to the Burlington Arcade; we were not long there and happily did not meet anyone we knew, for in spite of Ernest [aged twelve] drawing himself up to his full height, sporting a fashionable cane, a hat a little on one side and occasionally twirling an imaginary moustache, he looked very tiny and not the least like a chaperon. After that we had a brilliant idea and, all getting into a hansom, we bowled off to the Soho Bazaar. We saw some rather nice things there, I bought the most delicious little cooking apparatus, price one shilling and sixpence, it goes with methylated spirits, and I bought too a shilling frying pan to fit it.

Said goodbye to Bache and Herb and dear Dover Street, and dearest London and set off from Victoria Station by the Underground for Shepherd's Bush [to stay with Aunt Chatty]. No one to meet us, so we found our way to Netherwood Road. After knocking and knocking for about ten minutes Chats herself opened the door – they were in a regular scrimmage with only one servant in the house till tomorrow. After some time Vic and Flo [the faithful companions] appeared, collarless, cuffless, and covered with filthy old worsted jackets. I was so surprised about the house, it is so far nicer than I expected with nice comfortable rooms. It is much cleaner and brighter than Queen's Gardens though the house is smaller. We had tea soon after we came, a vague meal of bread and butter – neither very nice, and cocoa. We talked and laughed the whole evening, having great fun.

Thursday, June 24th, 1875

This morning I was quietly dressing in my room and thinking of nothing in particular when I heard someone calling me excitedly. I opened the door and Amy dashed upstairs, waving a letter and calling out, 'Ernest has passed *first of all!*' [into the Navy]. Hooray, hooray. You can imagine what rejoicing there was, how we all tore about telling everybody, clapping hands and shrieking with joy. The letter was from Aunt Maggie, of course awfully pleased about it. Everyone is so proud of him, it really is splendid. Fancy, first of all the sixty-eight boys who went up. We hurried over our breakfast and then dashed off to buy *The Times* and to telegraph the good news to Tom. It was in *The Times* – *E. Troubridge, first.* All Allen's boys who went up passed. How glad Mama and Papa would have been and how proud of him.

Friday, June 25th, 1875

Chats began wildly pumping me about religion, but I told her it was not the slightest use and laughed, so she was obliged to leave off. We went for a walk down the Uxbridge Road and found a vague little shop where a sale was going on and everything was too ridiculously cheap. We bought some little silk scarves for a penny three farthings each, brown and white and red and white spotted for ourselves, and black and white for Vic and Flo. Amy bought them each a very nice little apron, black and white, price threepence three farthings, and Chats a white silk handkerchief dirt cheap. I believe there were summer jackets for elevenpence, but we did not buy any. We also bought some very jolly artificial flowers, really good ones and so cheap. Amy bought eighteen dozen daisies for a ball gown, and I bought some for my hat.

We are astounded by the rudeness of the people about here, we hardly ever go out without being insulted – boys and men bawl things after us, chiefly about our height, which is nothing in the least out of the common, but as I say I don't believe a decent size person was ever seen before in the Bush. There is one set of boys who are always roaming about and whenever we meet them they sing out, 'Walking lamp-posts – there go the walking lamp-posts.' One bawled out to Amy, 'I'm sure that's a boy', and another said to me, 'There goes a man in woman's clothes.' One man ribaldly said as he passed me, 'I wonder how high ye'll be when ye done growing', and many more of the same sort are always happening, it is so annoying. *And* the way people *stare* at us, they stop when we have passed to watch us down the street, but that is not peculiar to the Bush, for in London too, we are *always* stared at. I think *men* are too *horribly rude*, the *way* they stare right in one's face, but even people in carriages did it, and people in broughams often poked their heads out of the window and remained staring for several minutes, sometimes we thought they might recognise us – but no, they were always strangers.

Wednesday, July 7th, 1875

In the evening we went to the most extraordinary concert given by emancipated slaves who call themselves *The Jubilee Singers*, in a Baptist Chapel called the Tabernacle. It was the last time they sing in London, so the place was crowded. They really sang very well indeed, but the most extraordinary wild nigger tunes and such dreadfully ribald *sacred* words, I don't think they ought to have sung them, and to me it seems funny to have a concert (for they had secular songs too and everybody clapped and laughed) in a consecrated building.

July 12th, 1875. Back home at Runcton

Such a detestable evening, Grobee actually made a fuss because I was writing my journal while the reading was going on. He not only makes us read a dry, stupid old book (which we do willingly to please him) but forbids those who are *not* reading to do anything which prevents them from listening. It is really too bad. Why should we be forced to listen when we don't want to? It is *his* book, dry and learned, all about Russian politics and campaigns of the beginning of the century, and we only read to him for his pleasure, therefore when we are *not* reading I think it *is* hard not to be allowed to do what we like. No one may move or speak a word the whole evening – it is most dull.

September 10th, 1875

To Uffington, Amy and I, with Uncle Sommy and Aunt Kitty, to stay with the Berties. Walked up to the house from Uffington station, met Lord Lindsey, such a dreadful old thing who does nothing but shake hands with everybody. He shook hands with us each three times before we got up to the house! It is lovely and filled with delicious things, lovely old prints and miniatures, pictures, china etc. Amy and I have the best bedroom, by mistake, which is so jolly. Next morning we laughed so because the room is full of looking-glasses so we couldn't find out where to place our baths. Mary [Bertie] showed us about the house – such a delicious ballroom where we had a game of battledore. On Sunday evening everyone sang hymns for three or more hours. On Monday we had such a jolly evening, we all went down to the hall and played Post and other games and then Sommy and Merthyr Guest danced ballets and breakdowns and Mrs. Bertie played. Oh, how we all laughed, then all the gentlemen tried to 'Shoe the grey mare', to balance a champagne bottle and all sorts of balancing feats, which was great fun as they kept falling down. Lord Lindsey was too splendid, he did nothing but make jokes and go into fits of laughter, and he would go and touch the people who were balancing and make them fall, altogether he thoroughly enjoyed it. At bedtime we two tore off to our room and there we tried to 'shoe the grey mare' and all the other tricks, for it is too 'show leggy', we could not do it downstairs. How we did flop about.

There was a little dance on the Tuesday but many people refused as it was such short notice and in the end it was only the people in the house. Now, you see, the worst of it was that we were seven dancing ladies and eight men counting Lord Lindsey, Mr Bertie, Monty – the little boy , and that wretch Hornige (Lord L's keeper), who of course were not much good, so in reality there were only four dancing men, at all events for the round dances. However, we had great fun and all danced tremendously in spite of feeble partners. To see Lord Lindsey and Mr. Bertie in the Grand Chain in the Lancers was the most lovely sight – they *would* go the same way as the women and we all got so weak trying to make them go right.

September 19th, 1875. From Runcton again

We heard something so nice today, Amy had a note from Aunt Maggie to say she was sending us three boxes of books and letters of Mama's that she has been keeping – she says till we were grown-up – but really I am sure she forgot all about them, for we have often asked her if she had anything of Mama's and she always said no. I do hope some of her drawings will be among them, how delightful it will be getting them, like something from another world, to see things of hers.

Tuesday, September 21st, 1875

Read history till eleven, went out in the garden, did German till lunch – what a wonderfully uneventful life we lead. Had a nice time putting up pictures and things in our room till eight-thirty, then read *Count Robert of Paris*. It is so funny, that book has taken quite a new turn and has now become very improper, isn't it dreadful? G. has only just woken up to the fact and doesn't like it at all, which I am very glad of, for now perhaps we shall read something else. We hate reading it out loud because it has no little improper bits that one could skip, like John Evelyn, but it is the plot itself, why, if it was not about so very long ago and if Sir Walter Scott had not written it, we should certainly never be allowed to read it.

September 22nd, 1875

Got up at seven as we were to breakfast at eight. I wore my black dress, as my white was not home (it never is when I want it), but Clem lent me her red sash and also a long white feather which I put in my daisied hat and made it look very nice. I forgot to say it was a most filthy day, pouring hard, so my dark dress did not look odd. Arrived at Norwich and off to St. Andrew's Hall for one of the concerts. Got tolerably good places, many people we knew were near us and Amy was close by.

The first thing, which was Mendelsohn's *Lobgesang*, was too lovely, Albani sang *most* beautifully, altogether that was delightful. Then came an interval of about ten minutes. Of course Amy and I got together directly and talked and laughed, we were just saying goodbye when Mrs. Birkbeck came and asked me to go home with them and stay at Thorpe [where Amy had been for a few days]. Of course I was awfully glad and accepted directly, it really was *very* kind of her and such fun for us. Eva is going to tell them to send my things directly, and so I hope they will come, for I cannot even dress tonight. Well, the second part, *Jerusalem* was very long and Madame Lernens Sherington, who sang, did make such dreadful faces. The third thing was lovely, but it was altogether rather too long. When it was over we were not long driving to Thorpe.

The house is most delicious and quaint, painted in very pre-Raph. colours, with matted and parquetried floors, old glass windows and tall wooden fireplaces, fitted with china. There are not many people staying in the house, among them a Mrs. Chapman, a youngish widow, we don't like her at all, she is so dreadfully put on, and I am sure she paints. Several people came to dinner, so it was rather dreadful my not being dressed, however I put on a white fichu of Amy's and a pink sash and did not look so very bad after all. After dinner Amy and lots of the party went off to *another* concert, Mrs. B. was tired so went up almost directly. Mr. Birkbeck and I had a very good game of Bezique till ten.

Yesterday I wrote how uneventful our life is, how little I thought that at that time tomorrow I should be playing a tête-à-tête game of Bezique with Mr. Birkbeck whom I have only seen once before.

Thursday, September 23rd, 1875

This is rather a nice house to stay at, everyone is so easy. Mrs. Chapman, who we disliked so, really is very jolly, so kind and good-natured. Amy and I do nothing but play the 'Chop' valse, which is a great gun here, they are all wild about it.

Friday, September 24th, 1875

Tom Hammond left this morning, rather a bore – a party without men is always rather slow. At eleven-thirty we set off for St. Andrew's Hall, Amy wore her brown silk, and écru and looked very nice. Mrs. Chapman was resplendent in a bright purple silk with here and there a touch of pale yellow, and bonnet to match with pale roses. She is so like a person in a book, the regular flaunting widow of forty, she has black hair very plastered down 'à la window curtain', very red cheeks and black eyes, a very flat tub-like figure with a very pinched waist – can't you see her? We found the hall crowded as the concert had already begun, we could not even sit together which was very tiresome. I got stuck next a tiresome old thing who would talk to her friend in the row behind while the singing was going on and who cried at Patti's solo, really cried with tears pouring down her cheeks and shaking with sobs – it was such a bore, but she did sing it beautifully. In the interval (which is such fun and ought I think to be longer) I saw and spoke to lots of people I knew. Kitty Birkbeck I saw in the most dreadful get-up, white, floating to the last degree – no attempt at tying back, with pink bows and a *tiny pink* silk bonnet, really it was bad enough to give one a nightmare. The second part was delightful too, and the end was splendid.

Lots of people at dinner, I sat next Mr. Birkbeck, who was very nice. He tried in every way to get out of me what Uncle Tum gave for the Lowestoft set (the one we found for him in London), of course I did not let it out and he was obliged to give in and confess that I was too sharp for him. Up to bed at eleven, my room is the dressing-room of Mrs. Chapman's and you can hear everything that goes on. We have long conversations some-times and tonight we opened the door and talked, she was most amusing. She was admiring my hair and saying how long and thick it was, she asked me what I did with it at night and I told her I left it down, then I said, 'What do you do with yours?' 'Oh,' she said, 'I put it on the table!' How we laughed.

Teusday September 28th, 1875. Back at Runcton

I finished *Jane Eyre*, I think it is perfectly *delightful*, Sunday, Monday and Tuesday every spare moment, every particle of time, I feasted on it and became perfectly buried, there is a weird mysteriousness about it that fascinates me, when I was not read-ing it I was thinking of it – it is real happy pleasure to me to read a book like that.

All Sunday evening Amy was learning part of the *Hymn of*

Praise, slow, sad parts – like low sobbing, and then getting quicker and quicker like yearning cries, then slower and dying away again, and all the time the same lovely air running through it. I was deep in *Jane Eyre*, at Thornfield with her – reading of her love for Rochester, her sorrow and then that scene in the garden, then their engagement – oh, how thrilling it was when their marriage day came nearer and nearer, yet one knew and felt certain that *something* would happen and prevent it. Oh, how awful and horrible it was, poor Rochester, one pities him so that one quite forgets his wickedness and then more interesting still his scene with Jane, his passionate pleadings, would she yield, or not? Could she have been mortal and held out, loving him as she did? Then his despair, hers, and that awful time she was wandering about, and all the time that air on the piano going on, now loud, now soft. Now I never hear it without going over it all again in my mind and feeling just the same as I did when I read it – I believe the impression will always last to a certain degree, and that I shall never hear that played without thinking of 'Jane'.

Saturday, October 2nd, 1875

This is the day Papa died, and we have now lived here eight years. How wonderful it seems that we have ever lived anywhere else, all the past and our other home life seems so like a half forgotten dream. One cannot realise that one was the same person then, it does not seem as if it was me, Laura, who lived with Papa and Mama at No. 8 Queen's Gate, and to whom all those memories belong. It seems as if it had all happened to someone else whom I have read of, and yet, it was really me.

Saturday, October 9th, 1875

Ever since we were at Uffington we have always been trying to remember the 'breakdown' Mrs. Bertie played, and we never could. Well, this afternoon Uncle Tum was quite alone in the Bank when he suddenly found himself *dancing* about to the very identical breakdown that we have been racking our brains to remember. He immediately wrote it down, played it when he got home and now Amy knows it too, isn't it jolly? It is a most delicious tune and makes you dance. I defy anyone to hear it and sit *quite* still. Coming home from Lynn Uncle Tum walked part of the way with us, he suddenly began humming it and we all joined in and in a few minutes we were all dancing about wildly on the road like maniacs – oh how we laughed.

Aunt Maggie came to stay, she gave us all nice presents and brought two lovely new Walter Crane books for us to see – such delicious ones. Oh, what would I not give to draw like that man, how I wish I knew him, I am sure he must be charming.

Wednesday, October 13th, 1875
At three the Valls. all came up to be drawn. We dressed them up as old-fashioned twinks [children], of the short-waisted period. They sat for us in groups and thought it great fun, they looked such darlings and sat very well. We are painting tiles as quick as we can, for we have such heaps of orders on hand, eighteen for Mrs. Birkbeck, sixteen for Aunt Maggie, three more for Aunt Bache, two for Aunt Amy, six for Mrs. Osborne, and an order in prospect for Mrs. Wicksted [Aunt Kitty's sister]. Besides all these we have an order for three yards of holland strip from Lilah Bertie, and a set of doilies for Lady Romney. Isn't it quite absurd? I wonder when we shall have done them all off. We mean some day to sell them to shops, but of course our orders come first.

October 21st, 1875
Home from Lynn by one o'clock and sank down in my room to *East Lynne* which I devoured till luncheon. I was wildly interested in it and I am ashamed to confess that after lunch I went back to my room (it was then two o'clock), sank down on the floor, curled up in a corner of my ottoman and never moved till I had entirely finished the book and it was past four – more then two hours bliss. I have another confession to make, *I very nearly cried*, yes, I never so nearly cried in my life, indeed I am not sure that *one* large tear did not roll down my cheek, but only

one, and I know I had a very large lump in my throat, but let not any girl of seventeen condemn me for a fool unless she has read it herself straight off as I did. It is such a hopelessly miserable book, so heart-rending. Poor Lady Isobel, her life was too dreadfully sad, and her death, I think, was the saddest of all. It was then, I think, that the one tear rolled down my cheek and I longed to cry. I really should have burst into tears (in spite of making my eyes red and the others noticing it) if Mr. Blakald had not known her and forgiven her before she died. That was the *one tiny* drop of comfort. But though I say all this still I see its faults, and they are many. The language in many parts is ridiculously stilted and affected, then Mrs. Wood has no sense of humour whatever, and it is silly of her to try and write comic scenes, but certainly the interest is kept up wonderfully, and that is the great thing.

After dinner read to Grobbins as usual. We finished Lord Makins' *Indian Empire* and have now begun an account of the Indian Mutiny of 1857 from the Annual Register of that year, which is very dreadful but interesting, of course, and nicely written. Such horrors as it describes, too horrible to be read out loud. We skip the worst parts, those massacres must have been awful – one can hardly believe it was such a short time ago.

We had planned a feast of blackberries and bread stewed in layers, so as we had a lot of cream we thought we would eat them together, but alas they were too disgusting, a cold shapeless purple mass, and there was that delicious cream longing to be drunk, but we *could* not drink it alone, so a bold attempt had to be made – Guddy we *knew* would not give us anything to eat at that time of night – so it was no use asking her, but then all the gobbits were in her power. There was only one thing to be done, to bag or go without, which of course was out of the question, so Amy and I set out on a marauding expedition. The others came too but kept in the background.

First we tried the larder, but alas that was locked, so we stole round to the other door. We heard Guddy talking volubly in her room, we stole past on tiptoe and made for the store-room, her room opens into it and the door was ajar, it was an exciting moment, but we could not go back empty-handed. I peered in, a large pot of blackberry jam was on the further table, I stole cautiously up to it, secured the prize and, clutching a few handfuls of ratafias on my way, we both rushed from the room back to the others and up to the school-room – triumphant! Plates and spoons were quickly produced and the large jug of cream and we each had a plateful, with an island of delicious blackberry jam in the middle. Doesn't it make your mouth water? I can tell you we were not long over it, and how we laughed and chattered – stolen fruit is always best!

Christmas Day, 1875

I feel I must write something about Christmas, though I haven't written for so long. The 'tree' is over, the boys are home, and the holidays have begun. I woke early, for me, and lay dozing in that delightful semi-conscious state I like so, but Stanbrook soon flounced in, wishing us a Merry Christmas, opening shutters, putting out the screen for our baths and clattering about, effectively disturbing my doze. We lay and talked a little, but Helen came and banged at the door in a great state of excitement and begging us to get up. I was last down and found everyone congregated round the school-room table, while on every plate was a pile of most delightfully mysterious parcels. 'Merry Christmas – Merry Christmas' called out everyone, then I added my contributions to the present piles and we all began to open. Such a noise as there was, such laughter, such screams of delight. It was too ridiculous, funny little presents they were – mostly boxes of choc. and crystallised fruits. I had a book I wanted very much, *Kate Coventry*. Chatty sent us some old music books, rather nice. Till church we spent our time in ruminating over our presents, eating choc. etc. Of course the church was decorated, large wreaths and festoons of holly and evergreens all about and devices in cotton wool, calico and coloured paper.

Of course we had a turkey lunch *de rigeur*, followed by the immortal plum pudding and mince pies. After luncheon we thought we would go and see Ellen Palgrave, who is ill, when the whole 'Valleyfield' party hove in sight across the Park, and the 'Rectories' down the Approach. By walking straight on the two armies met at our front door. They came to get us to go a walk with them, as we always do on Christmas Day, so off we set, sixteen of us. We went down the Lynn road, which is the correct thing to do, we met a great many holiday-makers like ourselves, but I don't think any seemed so jolly. Uncle Tum was in a very good mind and such fun, keeping us in fits of laughter. Coming home the boys larked about the fields, jumping hedges and ditches in the most ridiculous break-neck fashion, flying over hurdles into muddy ditches and emerging filthy but triumphant, much to the amusement of parties of Lynn cads. Uncle Tum joined them too and was quite as boyish as any. We parted at the Park gate and arrived home quite fagged and tired out, but rest was not to be thought of. The decorations were not finished for tonight and the little Christmas tree for Helen had to be done entirely.

December 31st, 1875. At Sculthorpe

The last night in the year, poor dear old '75. I am half sorry it is over, it has been such a quiet, happy, uneventful one for us. Really nothing important has happened, to us three at least. Ernest going into the Navy is a change for him and a real step, and Clem is now really engaged. Grandpapa is just the same and everyone else at home. We live at Runcton in our dear old way, thank God. *Outwardly* we are the same, whether *inwardly* I cannot tell. Only one hour more of '75, it's eleven o'clock now, and shall I tell you what we three are doing? Watching the Old Year out and the New Year in, of course.

Amy, Laura and Violet – in red dressing-gowns and floating hair, are disposed in comfortable attitudes, we two on the bed and Amy in the large armchair in Vi's bedroom. As the clock strikes twelve we are going to do a spell, alone, each in our rooms – eat an apple before the glass and, over your shoulder you will see *someone*. Of course I don't believe it a bit, and not being an imaginative person I am sure we shall see nothing. I had a long talk with Lawrence [Jones] today – a very grave talk, quite serious and solemn. I think he is – no, I won't say, for who knows how this journal may lay about, and I prefer to keep certain things to myself, though there is much I might say.

Our New Year's Eve night was the most dreadful sell I ever knew. In the first place our being together at all was only the result of many deeply laid plots, for Amy sleeps at the other end of the house near Aunt Bache, and with the incessant system of watching that always prevails here it was no easy matter for us to meet. Herb is always prowling about at all hours of the night and there is such a long passage to go down, of course she could not think of going back to her room again at past twelve, so she slept in my room instead. Why on earth there should be all this fuss about our going to bed and why we shouldn't talk together in our rooms I never can make out, for what could be more natural than our liking to spend the end of the Old Year together? However, such is the case and we had to manage accordingly.

Herb evidently scented something on hand, for Amy (who had said good night and gone quietly off to her room) heard him skulking about the passage, obviously on the watch, but luck favoured her. For one minute Herb went up to his study and at the same time Booba [the maid] came stumping up to bed, so directly she passed Amy seized the opportunity and fled on stockinged feet down the passage (under cover of Booba's heavy tread) and so arrived, breathless but safe, in Viddy's room, the little middle one over the porch, where we were already assembled. Chocolate was produced and we made ourselves comfortable, for it was not eleven yet. But here a most unfortunate contretemps occurred, Amy's watch was discovered to have stopped and the key left at home, however there is a large clock in the hall and that morning I had taken the precaution of asking Bache whether it struck the hours, and she said it did. So we thought we were quite safe as we could hear it ticking quite plainly. We set the door ajar, to hear it strike eleven, and talked in whispers, with fits of smothered laughter. But, oh, the scares we had, the footsteps and the doors we thought we heard. I think it is such fun doing anything secret of that sort. So we were very jolly, we had a nice Old Year's talk, discussing events – and people in particular. But meanwhile the time was getting on and we had not heard it strike eleven, though we felt sure it was past.

The house was quiet now, but for occasional snores from Booba's room above. Now a service of great danger had to be performed (for past eleven we knew it was, we thought it had struck while we laughed and talked) – someone had to venture downstairs to the hall to see what time it was. Of course I was that someone, armed with my candle, in my long scarlet cloak, white sleeves and collar and my hair hanging about. I stole silently downstairs, feeling rather like some tragedy queen stealing down to do some deed of darkness, while the others watched me from above. The great danger was that floods of light from my candle (and myself too when once down the staircase) were distinctly visible from the other end of the passage, where Herb if alarmed would make his first appearance. However, it was a necessity, so down I went, not making a sound, but suddenly a distant door creaked. In an instant Amy and Vi scuttled back to their room, making an awful noise, and I tore up as quick as possible – and after all it was nothing but a false alarm, so down I went again, for I was determined to do it, reached the hall and returned in safety. It was just half-past eleven.

We got everything ready, we stole about placing lights and bits of apple in each room and sat down to wait, talking softly with the door ajar. Now I must tell you that the Blue Room and the Pink Room, both large ones, are opposite each other and the Porch Room is in between. No one sleeps in the Blue Room (it looked large, desolate, cold and empty), and of course Vi and I meant to do it in our own rooms, but Amy was so nervous about it that she backed out of it at the last minute and begged me to go there instead, so I did. When we thought nearly half an hour had passed we bade each other farewell and each went to our separate rooms. We left our doors ajar, to hear twelve strike, and stood there waiting. I did not feel nervous, though the room was cold and cheerless, a high wind was moaning round the house and the ivy tapped against the unshuttered window in a weird mysterious way.

I stood there before the large glass, watching, all behind me was dark and shadowy and my face seemed to get more and more unlike me, a hollow cough sounded from the next room (where Stanbrook slept), but still I was not nervous and stood there very quietly, thinking . . . oh, of so many things. L. had said, 'I shall think of you as the clock strikes twelve.' I wonder if he did? But meanwhile time went on and not a sound was heard but the loud tick-tick of the clock in the hall and the whistling of the wind outside.

And so the Old Year passed away, for we never heard it strike, though we waited, listening intently. Though my thoughts had wandered quite from what I was doing, they were Old Year thoughts, mixed with some regrets, and though I did not hear it strike I felt suddenly that the Old Year was over and a New one had begun. I was filled with bright hopeful thoughts, and at that minute Amy called me softly outside. 'Wait a minute', I said, 'it is not time yet.' I was sorely disappointed, though it was a silly thing and I knew in my heart the time was gone. Five or ten more minutes we waited and then I went out on the landing, feeling sorry about it and yet glad too. Outside were Vi and Amy, more disappointed about it I think, than I was. 'Oh,' said Amy, 'I am *so* sorry it has been a failure.' Vi said, 'What shall we do, we have failed – it is too bad – don't you realise it?' 'I know,' I answered, 'I am sorry, there is nothing for it but to wish each other a Happy New Year,' and so we did and kissed each other warmly. A glow of affection came over us and we all felt merry, in spite of the failure of our little plan, so we went and sat all three huddled up on Vi's bed, for standing about so had made us cold, and there we had our New Year's talk.

We made a resolution that whenever we three were together, wherever we might be, on the 31st of December we would watch the year out and in together. We shook hands on it, and I hope we shall spend many times like that night. It is so delightful being three sisters, we are so free and intimate together, we never quarrel, if we have a little tiff – and even that is very rare – it never lasts long and when it blows over we are just as jolly as before. Amy and I are both hot-tempered, and I believe I have a talent for aggravation at times. I have a sharp tongue too, which is a very dangerous gift, indeed I do not think it is a gift at all, for it does much more harm than good – at least in my mouth. Why, I have even got rises out of Vi (about two in a year), which says a good deal for my horrid power of aggravation. However, as I said before, our squabbles never last long and are few and very far between, so they come more as gentle rousers than disturbances.

At about one, as we guessed, we separated. Of course as that old clock does not strike we could not really tell the hour. Amy and I went off to bed, saying good night to Vi. To bed, but not to sleep, we had so much to say, so many things to discuss that I should say it was near three before we finally turned our pillows and vowed we would not say a word more. Amongst other things we discussed men. Almost all of our limited acquaintance passed in review before our critical minds, and I am afraid few, if any, came unscathed from that ordeal – poor things! It is so odd to think that many, like Dor, Puny, Mort, Gee – or any of that sort, who do not know us the least, but think us good, rather humdrum little girls, possibly rather fun to chaff, have no idea how we discuss them and their conduct, how every little thing they do is noticed and commented on – what they said too, but not exactly from a love of gossip but more from love of studying people. That is a Troubridge trait and we all have it, and knowing and seeing so few people as we do we are obliged to make the best of our material and discuss those not very interesting personages, dissect their characters, show up their faults and failings and their good points, with more interest and at greater length than we should if we knew more.

It is now the end of 1875 – I wonder how I shall feel tomorrow night?

The End of Life at Runcton

Runcton, January, 1876
This book begins a new era in my Journals. I mean in future only to write occasionally. I have kept long Journals for every day till I am quite sick of them, I really have not the time to do it. So on the whole I think this present plan is best. I do not mean to detail every little event, but only the more important ones, and my thoughts about people and things connected with us and our life here.

Sunday, February 20th, 1876
It is just a week today since the fire at the Rectory. It was Sunday evening and we were calmly singing hymns in the Ante-room, very sleepy, as we always are after two services, when suddenly in rushed a troop of frightened people with white scared faces – they were Eva and Geoff, with sacks on their backs and all the little ones, laden with dolls. I don't think I ever was so amazed in my life. We could not imagine what had happened. I really thought they had gone crazy till they gasped out that the house was on fire and they had all come here for the night . . . A most interesting account was just going to follow but, alas for posterity, dinner intervened and a thousand other things, and now, a *fortnight* afterwards, I haven't the courage or inclination to write it, so instead I shall copy Amy's account from her Journal which, though most absurd and exaggerated, is true in the main facts and many details too.

The fire at the Rectory – February, 1876, by Amy
After dinner we were all singing to the organ as usual in the Anteroom when suddenly a great noise was heard and in rushed Eva, Winnie, Katy, Geoff, Aunt Ama and Chennie –

and Budding [the Nurse] in vague costumes, carrying lanterns and bundles, all talking at once at the tops of their voices. Never in the course of my existence did I feel so surprised, at last we made out that the Rectory was on fire and they had come here for shelter. They looked more like drowned rats than burnt out twinks, for their clothes were perfectly saturated with water which they had thrown over each other by way of helping to put out the fire which, by the way, turned out to have been in the roof and therefore not very alarming, especially as it had been put out before it had time to spread.

It happened as follows, the hour of dressing for dinner was come and the family party at Runcton Rectory had taken off their clothes when an alarm of smoke was spread. Uncle Willie seized some stray garment and rushed out to see a red light through the skylight in the hall. My beloved Aunt threw on her gown and appeared tearing towards a spare bedroom, she stopped at the door, seeing light within. Her lord and master threw it open – and behold the bed and ceiling in flames! Aunt Ama then flew down to the nursery with enormous presence of mind (and body), shrieking – Fire! Water! Fire! Ring the dinner bell! Two of her devoted sons instantly attacked the dinner bell, which they rang with the wildness of despair until the rope was broken by their noble effort. The servants and children heroically formed a line along the passage and nobly sacrificed their feelings by passing milk jugs and tea kettles one to another until the last Spartan hero emptied the contents on to the burning bed which, after an awful period of five minutes, ceased to blaze.

At this juncture the frail Eva, eldest daughter of the house, mounted the front stairs with a ladder in her arms. The devoted Rector proceeded, amid the tears of his protesting family, to mount the aforesaid ladder even unto the third step, from which elevation he proceeded to inject the garden squirt into a hole in the ceiling, thereby extinguishing the few remaining flames. Then, with one gallant rush, this Spartan family, accompanied by about twenty of the good villagers (whom the sound of the dinner bell had assembled), with one rush, I say, they entered the still smoking ruins, bearing every utensil for holding water which could be found in the house, filled to the brim. In one moment room – carpet—bed – Spartan family – devoted Rector and villagers were inundated with the blessed streams, and one long shout of thankfulness was sent up as they emerged wet to the skin. Twelve members of the Rectory family then arrived at the Hall, where they took up their abode for a week in consequence of this fatal disaster. (Much to the boredom of the school-room party at the Hall!)

Now I must tell you about our Art ventures, it is *too* delightful. Mortlock, instead of scorning us utterly is actually coming to terms. I have been looking back and I find there is nothing at all about it so I must begin at the beginning. Birdie Brett (a friend of Uncle Sommy's) took two of our tiles to Mortlock's for him to see. He admired them very much and said all sorts of absurd things about them, also he wrote off and asked us to design for him. Wasn't it an honour? Fancy loads of people employed in reproducing our designs – oh, Gloria! Well, we wrote back and said we were very willing and asked what he would give us for them. He answered we must fix our own prices, which put us rather in a hole, for we hadn't an idea what to ask. Of course it is all a dead secret from Grandpapa, who would forbid it instanter, but we consulted Uncle Tum and he thought five pounds for a set of twelve designs on paper. That is not quite half a sov. each. He said he did not really know what they were worth, however we thought that quite enough. Then of course we dawdled horribly over the designs, though we had only four each to do. They were all backgrounders, good, I think, and elaborate, but we had heaps of other orders on hand besides. At last nine were finished.

We had an uncomfortable sensation that we were going to be done, and some people said it was too much and some far too little, so at last we settled to ask Uncle Charles' advice, for he really understands that sort of thing. So we sent him the nine that were finished and determined to abide by his decision. He wrote by return of post, 'your designs are very good – ask two guineas each for them.' Then followed tremendous discussions, I was all for asking less – one guinea, I said, is quite enough, for we can do one in an evening, and we had really settled it so, for we thought it would be better to get less than to be shut up entirely. However, Ernest forbade us to ask less than two guineas, he said he would write to Mortlock himself, that it was shameful of us, that we were fools – donkeys – asses – and he was our brother and must look after our affairs. If we would ask low prices he should not allow it. So, at last, he persuaded us to let him write, but I confess I thought it foolish and horribly cheeky coolly to ask twenty-five pounds for a little parcel of twelve designs. However the letter was written and sent. He said, which was his idea too, that we could not separate the twelve designs, so if he did not like to take them all he must send them back at once, by return of post, which I thought rather rude.

A week passed, you can imagine how we were dying to hear. At last Mortlock wrote, that he liked them very much (wasn't it a relief?) and wished to know if the copyright was included in that price. Also he mentioned one which was on a plain ground and, he said, ought to cost less – (in which he was quite right for they take far less trouble or time) but not the least as if he thought the others too much. Wasn't it delightful, instead of the dreadful snub we expected?

Ernest wrote off directly for us, saying the copyright was certainly included, and enclosing a very pretty design Amy did which he might have instead of the plain one. Now he has written again, he wants us to enter into an agreement with him to supply no other shop. That requires some discussion. My idea is that we bind ourselves for a year or two, to supply him with designs if he will keep to his terms. Oh dear, isn't it delightful? Hooray! Hooray! Oh Jubilee! Fancy the honour and glory, our designs exposed for sale in a swell London shop. Of course we shall go and see them if we go to town.

Saturday, May 6th, 1876, in London

Shopped the whole morning – *flanéed* down Regent Street, shop-gazing with true country zeal. We got some ready-made black silk petticoats, rather nice, at a guinea. We decided to pay for these new toilettes with the money we have earned, so didn't want them to cost much. Oh what a bore it is being so poor. If only some good fairy would present us with a ten pound note each we could conjure up endless toilettes and really enjoy our Londoning, for it is a bore at seventeen to feel yourself a frump when you might look nice if you only had the means, and other girls seem to have so much – heigh-ho. However, it's no use whatever writing that nonsense, we are poor and poor we shall remain. Good fairies are, I'm afraid, extinct, and the only way to get hold of a little extra cash is to earn it.

After lunch we dressed and set off with Maria (Aunt Kitty's maid), first down Oxford Street, for our souls hankered after Mortlock's shop, and we longed to see our designs in the window. However we were doomed for a snub. Having screwed up our courage to enter without any professed reason (as we did not wish to tell them who we were), we vagued about the shop, seeing nothing whatever of our things but loads of other beautiful designs that made us tear our hair with rage, ours seemed so rotten after them – how Mortlock could take them! They told us they had none of modern children, so I suppose they have torn ours up. Felt cross, and our new shoes were so tight we could hardly walk, and they hurt awfully.

Wednesday, May 10th, 1876

Uncle Tum came to see us, raving about the Alhambra, which he said was the loveliest thing he had ever seen in his life. *Le Voyage dans la Lune* it is called, he gave glowing descriptions of it all and made us wild to go. He said the *danseuses* were so indecent in the Ballet that he would not take us, though he was longing to himself. *I* thought it far more proper for *us* to see women with next to nothing on than him, but I kept this opinion to myself. However, he is so longing to take us that I think we will be able to work him up to the right pitch.

May 10th, 1876

Stanbrook [their faithful maid] came to help dress the Ama [Amy – who was going to be presented by their great-aunt, Lady Cochrane], and we sent her out to get gloves. Cream-coloured shoes arrived and were discovered to be far too small, so we dashed about London the whole morning to try and find some. I don't believe any other girls who were going to the Drawing Room put their noses out of doors for fear of making them red. We got some shoes at last in the Burlington Arcade, dashed home and set to work directly at the dressing process. A. became hopeless over her hair, which she longed to do in little curls at the top, but everything would go wrong and it was getting late. Coiley (the grand dressmaker) was there and tried on her gown, which was much too big in the waist, so it had to be torn to pieces and made up again in a wild hurry. Those precious curls came right at last, Stanbrook attacked one side, Maria the other, while Amy gnawed sandwiches in the middle. Coiley and a 'young person' were clawing her gown, which was lying in a distended heap on the bed, and I surveyed the prospect from a neighbouring armchair.

At last she was dressed and looked *very* well. The petticoat was cream silk, covered with plissées and trimmings of cream net, long tunic body, square on the shoulders and laced behind, long train of cream-coloured grosgrain trimmed with net and bunches of cream-coloured primulas, long trails of which hung down the front and on the body, the curls appeared triumphantly up a'top, with feathers and a long tulle veil to finish. Round her neck she wore a thick silver Algerian necklace, *et – voila tout*. The whole effect was very 'tweet'. Aunt Kitty wore a plum-coloured silk, trimmed with gold and looked very badly, for of course her complexion cannot stand daylight. Sommy's get-up was very ugly, a cloth Court suit with gold. I watched them off from the window and heard the admiring comments made by a chorus of servants in the hall.

Eva appeared and we had tea and soon after the Drawing Roomites returned, looking cross, cold and bored, and dying for tea. Amy and I teased till Tumbo went off to the Alhambra to buy a box, so we skedaddled to our room, where I helped her out of her gown and talked it all over. A. said she didn't feel a bit nervous when it came to the point, and it went all right when the Lord Chamberlain bawled out, 'Miss Troubridge, presented by Lady Cochrane – kiss Her Majesty's hand.'

But to hurry on, we got neat for dinner, ate, and set off à pied for the Alhambra about eight-thirty. The first act was over when we arrived, but we stayed till nearly twelve, to the very end, and were perfectly enchanted. The ballets were too beautiful, particularly the Snow Ballet, when loads of girls dressed with snowballs and silver danced with arctic scenery all round and silver snow falling fast, while four little ballet girls dressed as swallows, in scarlet waistcoats and very short breeches, with dark blue swallow tail-coats, little blue and red wings made to flutter and swallowish caps on their heads, kept running in and out in the most lovely way – the only bit of colour in the whole thing, and their dancing was too wonderful. The lightness, the ease, you know. They had their hands in little red and white muffs which they kept up to their faces and rubbed from side to side in the most delicious way.

Part of the song they sing in that ballet is shivering as if they were all so cold. We got awfully excited, it was so mad. One song too we went crazy over, sung by a Frenchwoman dressed as a mountebank, she came in on a yellow car and sang this song, whacking on a big drum and blowing a horn in between in the most splendid way. She was encored three times. I could write very much more, for I haven't even mentioned the danseuses' legs, which were a sight to behold, with nothing on but tiny tarlatan frills and pink tights, not even drawers to speak of – however it's a delicate subject and had perhaps better be left unmentioned, more so as it is near twelve o'clock and I really must go off to bed. Just think of getting up tomorrow – too awful!

The next day we went again to Mortlock's with Birdie Brett

and went up to the painting room and asked about lessons we wanted to have. We then asked about the Miss Troubridges's tiles, without of course saying who we were. They said there were none ready but would we like to see the designs. We said yes, and they accordingly lugged out all our well known *chefs d'oeuvre*. Our behaviour was idiotic, for we became silly weak and did not admire them half enough, not at all at least. We really had not the face to admire our own things, but I think the woman twigged who we were.

Seeing the arrival of the Prince of Wales.

We hurried, elbowing through the rabble, and arrived breathless at No. 43 Grosvenor Place [the William Vernon's house] about four, found the balcony crowded with dreaders who had secured all the best places, tiresome fidgetty children and old maids. However we got into a nice corner with Gee and Tumbo and had rather fun. The streets of course were thronged, endless carriages, besides rabble. The Grenadiers' band passed shortly, playing so well, with a lot of soldiers and then came Life Guards. At about five we went in and had tea, and then back to our post. Waited an everlasting time and rumours of the most despairing nature reached us, that the Prince had only just reached Portsmouth, that he would not reach London till eight, and so on. However we waited patiently and at about six o'clock mounted policemen rode down and stopped the traffic till all the streets he was to pass were cleared. Then the Grenadiers marched up and lined the streets – ten paces apart on either side – all the way down, which had a very pretty effect. Then more waiting and it got horribly cold. At last about seven o'clock faint shouts were heard in the distance and the train of carriages with their escort came in sight. Everyone stood up and hoorayed and shouted and waved their handkerchiefs as they passed. The Prince looked very well, quite tanned and not so fat. The Princess and their two sons filled the carriage. The Prince looked straight at our balcony and recognised Uncle Tum. He waved and nodded to him.

May 17th, 1876

Went to the Court Theatre to see *A Scrap of Paper*. The piece was delightful, I enjoyed myself awfully (as usual), it was so exciting and beautifully acted. The later piece, *A Quiet Rubber*, was wonderfully good too. Hare acted a very, very old man, Lord Kildare, in the most extraordinary way. He was the boy in the last piece, and the transformation seemed too wonderful. His face looked about a hundred, and his hands a million – all twitched wrinkled and stiff. It was a splendid piece of acting but almost horrible, it was so life-like, so like Grandpapa when he was silent and speechless with rage. (This was the last night of our London season and we felt very sad as we really have had a perfect time.)

December 31st, 1876

I am so sorry poor old '76 is over, it has been such a jolly year for us that I must write a farewell, even though the spirit moveth me not. Let's see what has happened all this year – nothing very important. I have grown about three years older in the one, N.B. not in looks – 'Coming out' did that, I suppose. I never was very shy, but now it has washed off my horizon altogether. I enjoy *everything* pretty well, I mean everything that could possibly be enjoyed. I can flirt now and have amused myself a good deal in that way. Last year this time I believe I fancied myself in love – a great mistake and I never mean to again. I have discovered a cavity in my left side instead of a heart. I much prefer it so and hope it will remain, yet I'm awfully fond of men, I like 'em all – such dears.

I am trying to think over any change since '75 – have I got anything new? I can only think of one thing – a waist! I don't think I had one last year. I've a lot of new frocks too in the natural course of events, and would have a lot more too if I had my wish. We have all become ten times vaguer, ten times larkier and ten times jollier and more improper than last year. We are just as twinkish [childish] in the way of tearing spirits, and make more row than ever. We are now great guns among all the boys about, George – Cressie – Mort – Gee and Wal are all devoted,

but especially Cripps [Cressie], who is supposed to be wildly
spoony on me, he is the greatest fun. He is at Oxford now and in
the summer vacation when Clem and Helen were at Hunstanton
for a month or more he used to walk over here four or five
times a week 'to take care of us' when we had no chaperon, and
we used to stroll about together and have charming little tea-
parties.

We have taken to smoking lately, George gives us cigarettes
and we like 'em no end, that is Amy and I. She is prettier than
ever and a thousand times wilder, everyone admires her and lots
of men make up to her. She wears her heart not even in her side
but well on her sleeve and is in and out of love twenty times.
Such a tenderness for Charley – such a tenderness for dear little
Ogle etc. etc. – she amuses me.

Art has not been neglected, our tiles have improved, besides
our dealings with Mortlock. That old duck Clem is as jolly as
ever, but she is getting so dreadfully fond of Willy [Wright] that
I know she won't be able to resist marrying him much longer –
what shall we – and the poor infant – do without her? By the by,
that little body, Helen, has cheered up wonderfully lately. She is
very amusing and has all sorts of jokes with the boys when they
come to see us. Geoffrey, Dor, Puny and Harry are great friends
of ours too. Dor [Uncle Hay's son] is simply too delicious, he
came here for the Sandringham Ball and stayed on nearly a week.
We have begun a new system this year of soirées with the people
we like who are staying here, held round the school-room fire,
generally from ten or eleven till one, when we roast chestnuts or
toast, eat chocolates, or if everything else fails eat bread and
cheese, and chatter and laugh and gossip and smoke in a most
friendly way. Dor came every night and was the greatest fun, only
he would come with less and less on every night and loll about,
occasionally becoming very improper, much to our amusement
and edification. Puny is good fun too at soirées, telling amusing
stories and singing comic songs.

We had some killing female soirées, masquerade ones, when
Dulcie Pearce and Mary Upcher were here. I thought they might

be getting dull one night so came swaggering into Dulcie's bedroom, where they all were, in an ulster, revealing the immortal check trousers, high choker and spotted tie, a little forage cap on one side, and a burnt cork moustache and eyebrows, eye-glass and cigarette. They nearly exploded with laughter and Dulcie, looking too disrep. – half undressed with her hair floating about threw herself into my arms, calling me her *darling* Captain! Then we gave a series of masquerade soirées, which ended with a ballet danced by she and I on her last night. She wore pink silk tights, an apology of a skirt, bare neck and arms, bejewelled and floating hair – I never saw anyone look so disrep. I appeared in black tights, very short scarlet knickers, tight olive green cuirasse, gold band and collar, velvet cloak on one side, my hair made to look short, and my moustache. Amy and Vi played the *Voyage dans la Lune* and we came in hand in hand dancing. Clem was there too and they all fell flat on their faces in shrieks of laughter, which resounded through the whole house (it was about eleven p.m.), so much so that Guddy [the housekeeper] came upstairs raging to know what was up. I flew to the door and locked it just in time, and we blackguarded her through it till she went away, when we began to dance again.

We have been out a good deal on the whole this year and had a great deal of fun, more than I ever had before – all but poor Vids who has not come in for many larks. The boys are getting on very well at Wellington and the *Britannia* I have settled my ambition, which is novel writing, which I occasionally have mad rages for – but don't mean to take it seriously yet.

December 31st, 1877

In my heart I feel there will be a great change before I write again – before '78 is gone – with cold and heat, burn and freeze. Shall I write from here then I wonder? But I did not mean to peer on ahead, a retrospect was what I meant to write. London was our first real fun this year – Amy wrote it all. It was fun detailing it, like thinking over a delicious dinner, delightful occupation if you have starved since – but if you have eaten – oh, a great many nice things since – some even very nice – it cloys you somehow.

To think of that darling Ernest, we do so long for him, his heavenly old face, his hair – the delicious clottedness of it, his angelic blue sausage body – I can't think of him, I hate it, it makes me long to see him so. This is the first Christmas we ever spent away from each other. I suppose we shall get used to being without him, and what a difference it makes when one knows he is happy and jolly. This looks so wildly bookish written . . . I must shut up.

1878

All along 1878 has been remarkable for engagement, but the crowning point was reached when an engagement, real and bona fide, actually came off at Runcton, when George Cresswell proposed to Conny Gurney here, in this very room. Oh wonders will never cease, something has happened here at last, in this poor old sleepy hollow. She accepted him too. What a gay time that was, we all went to the wedding, such lots of presents and a nice little house in King Street, Lynn, ready and waiting for them, Amy was chief bridesmaid, Hugh Barclay best man.

1879

The year began sadly enough, with poor Conny's death – six weeks after the wedding. Her funeral was here – in our church-yard. How cruel it seems, how *utterly* incomprehensible. She was the first of our friends, of our generation to die – that is the first we knew and cared for, which made it all the harder to realise.

Nothing occurred of any interest for some time, Tom was gazetted and joined his regiment, the 1st Battalion of the 60th Rifles at Winchester. I went abroad in the spring to Dinard, to stay with the Willie Davys, and had great fun. Lots of tennis and French cakes, also expeditions to Mont St. Michel and Dinan, long walks through lovely woods full of wild flowers, besides good musical parties.

May, 1879

Go to the doctor about my eyes. First time I had seen a doctor since I had the measles ten years ago, bar being re-vaccinated five years ago! I have to bathe them and wear a patch and only read or write using one. Spent a day at Hunstanton to see *our* house.* We saw over it and liked it, it looked so nice and neat. Had the bright idea of substituting a volume of Byron and reading *The Bride of Abydos* aloud to Grandpapa instead of Cowper's *Task*, etc. which 'the Ancient' had chosen. He only said, 'There is no one like Cowper,' so no harm was done! 'The Ancient' is getting rather vague now but we are not allowed to contradict him. When he says, 'Amy dear, you remember the battle of Waterloo, darling?' an enthusiastic answer has to be given, 'Oh yes, Grandpapa, how exciting it was when the news came!' But it was not so simple the time he thought he had been made a peer and sacked all the old servants because they did not call him 'My Lord'.†

It became really awkward when he used to order the carriage and say he must go to London to take his seat in the House. We sisters tried to dissuade him for various reasons – it was too cold, or too wet. But he said, 'I do not want to fail in courtesy to the little Queen.' Then one morning he came down to breakfast and greeted me, the first to appear, by saying, 'I think it went off well.' I answered 'Yes, Grandpapa, I'm sure it did.' Vi came down next, to be greeted with, 'It was a success, I think?' I signed that I had no idea what it was all about, so Vi also agreed that it was a great success, and the same was said to Amy, all to our great mystification until at last he said, 'I mean my maiden speech in the House and I think at my advanced age the dear little Queen will not expect me to go again.' He had very mercifully dreamt it.

June, 1879

Went to London – new Frock, new jacket, new gloves, new

---

* Where we were to live when we had to leave Runcton.

† I don't know if there had ever been an idea of this when he was very rich before the Gurney crash.

hat, new boots, how ridiculous! Met Amy and had quite a gay visit to Abbey Lodge, doing lots of plays. Uncle Hay failed us for a play party. Too late to reap up anyone else, de Bunsens all going out, so Tanner [their maid, Stanbrook] was tweaked up in a cap as our 'Aunt'. She rather gave the show away by dashing forward to open the cab door!

Went to Shepherd's Bush. Oh, horror – stinking underground, blacks and cads, arrived reeking and half suffocated to lunch with Aunt Chatty, Vic and Flo, and Charlie Walrond. Saw their new house.

June 30th, 1879

To tea with Tardy [Orde], met Oscar Wilde, the poet. Both fell awfully in love with him, thought him quite delightful.

July, 1879

To the National Gallery, saw Sarah Bernhardt there, had a good stare at her. Met Tardy and went together to tea at Oscar Wilde's – great fun, lots of vague 'intense' men, such duffers, who amused us awfully. The room was a mass of white lilies, photos of Mrs. Langtry, peacock feather screens and coloured pots, pictures of various merit.

To Mansell's, saw the man who will write about my drawings soon, I think it is safe. To Mortlock's – rather fun, he says he will take anything we send him and is longing for more of our designs. We mean to go home and paint and pay off a few of our confounded bills.

August 15th, 1879

My birthday of twenty-one, a very, very dull day, eyes very weak, felt miserable, did nothing. Uncle Sommy is going to give me a guitar for my birthday, one that belonged to Grandmama, done up.

In October and November took place our never-to-be-forgotten visit to St. Michael's Mount, and our delightful friendship with that darling Lill [St. Aubyn]. I should not have thought it possible to love any girl so much who was not one of us three. She, Amy and I are all three the very best of friends. Had a wonderful time at the Mount, with boating, fishing and sailing, but rather a vague journey down as we were told by a porter that our train stopped twenty minutes at Newton for tea, and were gorging in the refreshment room when the train went off without us! Oh, horror, no other train to Penzance, telegraphed to Plymouth to stop Tanner and the luggage, on to Plymouth to an hotel for the night, rather fun.

December, 1879

Had a letter from Mansell asking for designs for Christmas and New Year Cards. Mean to work hard and get a little cash. On December 12th finished my first design, drew at the cards every day till the 20th.

December 31st, 1879

Vi and I alone at home [Runcton], bar Helen, who has gone to bed. Amy is at Keswick, Tom at Winchester (his long leave was up yesterday), and darling Ernest still far away at sea. Heigh-ho, we six are well scattered. Oh, to be all six together here once more. I can still see and feel around me the familiar landmarks and well-known nooks and corners of our *dear, dear* home – Runcton. Twelve years and more now have we lived in and loved the dear old place. How little did we, or anyone else, think when all those years back we found here a refuge and a new home – six poor little orphans as we were – that time would pass and find us still here, year after year, till now we stand able and ready to fight our own battles and take care of ourselves when the much talked of, long dreaded time shall come that will exile us from Runcton and send us out to make a home for ourselves elsewhere.

I have just looked at the clock, only one hour is left of '79. I shall cease writing as we must have our New Year's Eve talk. Would that we were all here together – good-bye old journal for another year. Where shall I write from next?

1880

On May 28th Amy and I went to London to Abbey Lodge, nearly missed the train because we were madly trimming hats till just before we left. It rained a lot but we had various gay doings, plays with Tom (up from Winchester), the Leghs, St. Aubyns etc. Invested in some *toques*, which are *the* thing to wear now. Met Bea and Tivo [Rachel Gurney] who were coming to tell us that Uncle Hay had been telegraphed for as Grandpapa was so ill. Felt horrified and very down about it. He was better a few days later, but on June 14th, very bad news from home, felt very miserable, so startling after the very good account on Saturday. Stayed in a long time, expecting a telegram to summon us – none came, so went out, lunched out, back at four. Found a telegram, *Come at once*, too dreadful, left by the five train, met Uncle Hay at St. Pancras and travelled home. Heard all was over at Lynn, felt stunned and shocked. He died in the afternoon, quite quietly and peacefully and felt no pain – could not realise it at all.

Aunt Kitty, Aunt Maggie and Uncle Sommy were at Runcton, all very kind to us. Poor Helen so glad to have us back to comfort her, and Vi arrived from Keswick the next day. Oh, what a meeting for we three. At home again, and yet not our home now.*

Aunt Bache was delightfully kind, she did suggest our living with them, also that we should separate, but it is really obvious to everyone our only chance of happiness is to live together and alone, so I think it will be Hunstanton. Talked with Aunt Minnie, she was so kind about our having furniture and things from here.

One of our difficulties was no spoons and forks. When asked, Uncle Sommy was so vague and only said that everything had been sold from Queen's Gate when our parents died. It was Durnford, the butler, who saved the situation (he had been butler to our father who had relinquished him to *his* father-in-

* Runcton was to be inherited by Uncle Hay, the eldest son. He was over sixty, was in the Bank at Norwich and had lived all his life that side of Norfolk so rather naturally did not want to move. Then the Lynn Bank wished Uncle Sommy to live there, so Uncle Hay sold the house and some of the land to his brother.

Laura's first pastel portrait, of her two-year old daughter Jaqueline in 1891. It was the success of this painting that made Laura take up portrait-painting as a way of adding to Adrian's somewhat modest salary as Secretary to the Great Ormond Street Hospital for Sick Children.

Cyril Wilde by Laura, 1891. It was after seeing this portrait of Oscar Wilde's elder son that Queen Victoria commissioned Laura to paint several members of the Royal Family. Constance Wilde was a cousin by marriage of Adrian Hope who was later appointed guardian to the two boys after Wilde's trial.

*Laura's portrait of H.R.H. Princess Victoria Eugenia (Ena) of Battenberg, later
Queen of Spain, in 1892. "I do squeak when they curl my hair," Princess Ena
confided in Laura, "and now you are here they curl it three times a day!"*

H.R.H. Princess Beatrice of Battenberg, the second of Laura's series of Royal Portraits painted at Osborne in 1892. Prince Henry would stand beside Laura and say, "Yes, Mrs Hope, yes - but the Princess is larger," followed by the Princess's, "Oh, Mrs Hope, not so large please!"

law to save him from the drunken butler!). He came to Amy and told her he had taken a chest of plate to Coutts Bank in 1867, so she concocted the following letter, *Miss Troubridge presents her compliments to Messrs. Coutts and would like to know when and by whom the chest of plate was removed which was deposited at the Bank in October 1867.* By return of post came a letter to say it was still there! When it arrived, great excitement, our wildest hopes fulfilled by lots of awfully nice real silver things. Unpacked, examined and gloated!

August 29th, 1880
Our last Sunday here as our home – all felt dreadfully down. Said good-bye to all the old servants and to Runcton as our home for ever. [We then stayed about – as our house was not available till November.]

November 17th, 1880
Got the key and explored our house. The first step towards preparations was taken – the chimneys were swept. Discovered a most delightful loft to make into a studio. Cashed a cheque, which Mrs. Lee Warner showed me how to draw. Amy, when first writing out cheques spoilt ever so many by copying Mrs. Lee Warner's signature! I, being more practical, went to the bank and got on very well until the clerk said, 'How will you have it, Miss?' Completely flummoxed, I said, 'Oh, er . . . in one of those brown paper bags.' Audible titters from the clerks and poor me covered in confusion.

We had been given our bedroom furniture from Runcton, also our maids' rooms and kitchen things, so only had to furnish the drawing-room and dining-room. We were given a hundred pounds of our own money and went up to London with this in a bag. We began by seeing Irving at the Lyceum and fell in love with his wonderful flame colour velvet curtains, so decided we must have the like for the drawing-room. This, although not a large room, had a big bow window so needed a fair amount of curtain material. We found out where Irving's velvet came from and got some, quite undeterred by the fact that it was silk velvet and ten shillings a yard, only eighteen or twenty-two inches wide. We wanted a ceiling paper and saw one with gaily coloured humming birds but thought its white ground dull, so we had some made in Paris with a gold ground. The walls of the room were orange with a dark wooden dado and mottoes painted round the cornice. The carpet was plain brown velvet pile. We also spent five pounds on a coffee set, but later decided we could not afford coffee after dinner! All this sounds rather silly, but we did not regret it for Hunstanton was a very bleak, drear place, especially in winter, and our little room with its amazing ceiling and bright glowing walls and curtains was a great comfort.

Hunstanton, London and Engagement

March, 1881 [Hunstanton]
After lunch, rouged, curled, doeskin-gloved – these metaphorically, mind you, sallied forth to pay some calls – loathesome. Joyfully and thankfully thrice did we hear the glad tidings, 'Not at home', and shoved in our cards. On March 4th the gold ceiling paper was put up, to the astonishment of the local inhabitants.

May, 1881
Hear that it is settled that Uncle Tum and Aunt Kitty are to live at Runcton. Later that month go to Keswick for a dance, which we enjoy. Felt almost quite happy being with trees and flowers again.

September 29th, 1881
A lovely day, Mr. Elwes arrived at eleven, with loads of parcels, beaming, armed with a large box from Charbonnel and Walker's, and a barrel organ. He helped us to hang lanterns and get things ready for tonight. A most successful champagne picnic on the rocks. Fenwicks, Greens, George Seymour etc., etc. – shrimping – cricket – boating – finished with a cold collation for ten, and a dance to the barrel organ at the Castle (our nickname for our little house).

November 24th, 1881 THE DAY
Tom went up to London by early train, to come back with Ernest. Drew all the morning, hockey all the afternoon. Suddenly at five a telegram from Ernest to say he arrives at nine that same evening – having missed Tom in town. Wild excitement, telegraphed Amy to come by first train tomorrow. Limpet [Helen], Vids and I tearing about, getting the room ready and seeing about

things. This included putting up every flag we possessed (mostly upside down!). At nine down to the station, a dark windy night. He arrived – breathless excitement (he was hiding in the Guard's van at the extreme end of the train). Such an evening! All tremendously happy, only wanting Tom and Amy to be humanly perfect – he loving the 'Castle'. Could hardly believe it was not a vague dream that Ernest was home at last. He had been at sea four and a half years, and was now nineteen.

To Lynn for the day, many friends and relations to see Ernest, who became a sort of Mart Show in the Tuesday Market Place, we girls doing the admiring show-women. The next day we had a dinner party of ten and then a little dance with a pianist from Lynn. Ernest has taken to rousing us very early by rushing round the house calling, 'Show a leg!' as from a hammock.

December 23rd, 1881

Arrived at Runcton – but the whole thing seemed so strange and unreal – the Valls. and Valleyfield, and yet Runcton.

December 31st, 1881

A misty dull day, the Old Year dying out in a subdued sullen way, sorry for its misdeeds perhaps. Back to Hunstanton – a cheery dinner *à trois* and a quietly nice evening.

January, 1882

I went on to Hopton and for the first time we ever remember we all six sleep under different roofs – Helen at Runcton, Ernest at Stoke, Tom at Long Stratton, Vi at Keswick, myself at Hopton and Amy at Sculthorpe. There is a Fancy Ball at Dunstan, near Norwich, and Ernest is going as our great grandfather, Sir Thomas Troubridge, Rear Admiral of the White, 1799, with white silk stockings and breeches, buckled pumps, short-waisted long-tailed ancient uniform coat with huge flaps in front, lace stock and shirt frill, the Order of St. Ferdinand on a pale blue ribbon, sword, an immense cocked hat and epaulettes and curly powdered hair. Vi goes as a Vivandière of the last century, tricoloured striped petticoat, red satin coat with white waistcoat, silver buttons and braid, lace apron and jabot, a *tonneau* [small 'barrel' of brandy], powdered hair and three-cornered hat. The next day Ernest came to Hopton full of the Fancy Ball. He elaborately described the whole thing and all the dresses I wanted to hear about. One comfort was his costume was declared to be far the best of the men, and Vi's of the ladies – rather a triumph. I felt pleased, especially as to the latter as it was designed by me. He said Vi looked lovely and was much admired.

February, 1882

Staying at Ollerton, walked to a church a mile off. A hopeless barn with an old owl who mumbled through the service and endless sermon. Runcton Church rises to a glorious Cathedral, and Uncle Willie to a veritable St. Paul. Reflection on the visit: result of a few days experience in a house with four babies and thin walls, that it's always somebody's turn to shriek! As usual, cold and uncomfortable prayers in a dinnery, fireless dining-room.

Amy and Vi come back to Hunstanton after a visit to Abbey Lodge full of delightful things to tell, like two uncut books. They went to two picture galleries, a circus, a dance, a dinner-party and three plays in the four days – not bad!

Buckled to and had a really energetic morning, and most loathsome it was, a regular premature Lenten morning, kneeling for three hours on the bare boards of the studio floor, with back-ache, arm-ache, leg-ache, and a placid smile, measuring and drawing out the diamond pattern on the floor, Amy meanwhile painting the same.

Ash Wednesday

To church, only the Litany and that superannuated, harsh, impossible Commination Service, which we three listened to in silence. Vi and I hard at work finishing the studio floor, then I drew the whole morning. Thank goodness have nearly drawn out the most difficult, the really only difficult design in my new set of illustrations for a book of *Little Thumb*. [the first book she illustrated]. There are seventeen figures in it, some small and hard to draw.

A lovely day, went out till dinner on the beach, a wonderful glorious sunset, with an opal sea perfectly calm, stealing in in ripples among the dark rocks, the pools all reflecting the crimson sky. Quite pleasure enough to look and live and breathe on such a day. This weather gilds everything we do in our peaceful humdrum life and makes it all twice, ten times as happy.

Went for a walk in the Le Strange's park, for once among woods and birds, felt as if we were at home again it was so like Runcton. Could not walk there often, felt very sad, and almost glad to get back to the sea and cliffs and hovels of Hunstanton that cannot raise a thought or memory in one's mind.

A delightful letter from Tardy [Orde], asking me to go abroad with them in the summer. It would be too perfect – money is the only difficulty, and I might possibly overcome it with my favourite weapons – pencil and brush. Felt it would be a happiness to go.

April, 1882

Ernest has a week's leave from Greenwich, so away with all the furniture, a general illumination of Chinese lanterns, and at nine a loud-playing, joyous piano organ we had engaged in the afternoon arrived, with two Italians (Cockneys probably) in charge. We established them at the garden door and had a wild dance for about an hour, everyone rather mad, the piano organ playing furiously, frantic polkas and schottisches, also one figure of a quadrille to which we danced the Lancers very quickly straight through without stopping once. Nearly died of laughing!

Good Friday

Hot Cross Buns to begin the day, overhauled my hats, past and present, an unpleasing occupation. Endeavoured to build fresh edifices from the ruins of several battered old friends, but didn't accomplish much. Demolished several and only finished one new one. The subject is getting serious – painted a little and felt much soothed.

Amy and I spend the day in Lynn. Walked up to Runcton through the Long Walk – everything looking, oh so lovely – and like home. It can't be quite wrong to covet your neighbour's garden when it was yours once.

June, 1882

Amy and I at Abbey Lodge. Trimmed our new hats, and off by the 12.30 to Maidenhead, Marie (de Bunsen), we two and Lothar de Bunsen, *her* first cousin. He is christened the 'R.L.C.' – Royal Licensed Chaperon – nobody knows why, as he is not even a cousin of ours. We fell awfully in love with Maidenhead, it is simply charming. Paddled about in a delightful little canoe and thoroughly enjoyed it. I love the easy, happy and perfectly independent feeling of 'paddling your own canoe'. Back to London, quickly dressed, then Lancer [Orde] arrived to dinner and we went *à trois* to a French play, to see Sarah Bernhardt in *Le Sphinx* – so ghastly, a dreadful story. Sarah looked very well in lovely dresses.

Heard the surprising news that our cousin Eva [Gurney] is engaged to the widower, George Cresswell. It is so sudden somehow and difficult to realise them as lovers – we are wildly interested.

August, 1882

Amy and I have a jolly visit to Moor Park, to Mrs. Bateman and her son Lee, then very devoted to Amy. He is a great performer on the banjo. There we met Jo Joliffe, a new man – cheery and wears an eye-glass. Much enjoy canoeing on the river.

November, 1882

We sisters, Tom, Lee and Lancer all go to the Swaffham Ball. Had a delightful time, danced wildly the whole time – got back at nearly five, having danced the ball out. Amy and I go to the Welbys, for some theatricals. This was the first time I was to act in Gilbert's play *Sweethearts*, with a young American, Douglas Grant. Felt in a *deadly* fright – two hundred people looking on, but it was all right when the curtain went up and I was once started. Wore my white high frock with pink ribbons and buckled shoes. Mr. Grant acted *beautifully*. I should have been nowhere if he had not done it so well, but I liked acting with him. Wore black velvet for the second act, with Marie Stuart cap of old lace and my hair curly-powdered, lots of diamond rings, and black round my eyes to make me look sad. Everyone was too heavenly to me when it was over and said it had been awfully good. There was a second performance the next night but rather a sticky audience who evidently thought it vulgar to laugh, and only sniggered into their pocket handkerchiefs.

December, 1882

Longed for more daylight to paint by. Think of the hundreds of summer afternoons, long lingering days, when I might have painted and have *done nothing* to last – I *wish* I wasn't such a hopeless *dabbler* in art – a feeble dilettante.

December 27th, 1882

Vi and I go to Sculthorpe, where Douglas Grant joins us and *Sweethearts* is acted again – with much success, in spite of Herbert Jones as the gardener not knowing a word of his part!

December 31st, 1882

The last day of poor old '82. Felt sorry, for it has been a good year to us and we have had many good times together. A wet day, too, a day of ceaseless rain. '82 positively wept itself away . . . Music in the evening and talk, disturbed by the dying year, watching for its waning, talking over what it had brought us and thinking the rest. We talked of it with varied feelings and I think perhaps I was the most loath to let it go – but, sorry or not, the Old Year died at twelve and we opened the window to let in '83, wished each other all good wishes and drank healths in mulled claret, especially that convenient toast – *les absents*. Then to bed.

1883

At the 'Castle' [the Hunstanton house] the dining-room is finished and a great success. White wooden dado, all woodwork white, a rich gold, green and red stamped leather paper, and Lothar's gift – the old oak chimney-piece in all its glory.

February, 1883

All the house astir with preparations for Ernest's departure. We said good-bye with light hearts, for he will be back in England in May at latest, and so we are spared parting with him for years as we feared. The fact is we Troubridges are too precious and scarce to be so scattered – when there are only seven all told.

May, 1883

Depart for London [to stay with the de Bunsens at Abbey Lodge] – Amy, myself and the ever faithful Tanner. Much shopping, lunched lightly on strawberry ices and our old friend Bath Bun Esq. at Grainger's, after to the Grosvenor Gallery – spent about two hours looking at the pictures, a dinner-party and after a 'drum' – lots of people we knew – enjoyed ourselves. Next day, to the Royal Academy, spent hours with the pictures and found out our favourites. In the afternoon to the Aquarium and saw the Wild Horses. Next day, to the Park with Uncle Tum to see the Drags Meet. It was very amusing, strolled about the Park amongst the crowds of people – saw lots of friends. Walked to the Fisheries Exhibition, thoroughly enjoyed it – *flanéed* about among the things and sat and listened to the band in the dear old gardens, the Horticultural (where we used to play as children). In the evening to German Reeds Concert Party – Corney Grain most amusing. Another lovely day – but alas, alas, some dreadful news for us which sent us post haste down, down to the very depths – darling Ernest sailed yesterday, having been appointed to the 'Satellite' – with only one day's notice, and we shall not see him again for two years. We felt crushed, and shopped in a sort of limp way.

June, 1883

In the afternoon went to Hurlingham in two hansoms with

Charles and Lancer [Orde] – polo and a band and lots of people, the garden lovely. Went to see the Gemmells about the exchange of our Hunstanton house and their London one in Gloucester Street [Victoria] – liked them so much, nice elderly women who paint (pictures *bien entendu* – not their faces) – and such a nice little house. Spent a delightful day, clear sky, sunshine, at Ascot. We set off in our smart cream and striped frocks, with the faithful Jo Joliffe, went to the Deichmann Drag where Lancer met us and presently Capt. Thornton came and introduced his pal Capt. Stopford, and off we went to lunch at the Guards' Tent. Met loads of friends and amused ourselves. Sat on the Drag to watch more racing – won some gloves! Tea and strawberries in the Guards' Tent.

Left London for Hunstanton to get the 'Castle' ready for the Gemmells, and on the 22nd – off, bag and baggage to London – thirty-two packages in all. Arrived safely at Gloucester Street and there had rather a *mauvais quart d'heure* – two horrible gaunt men, clothed in rags, got into the house and insisted on taking our luggage upstairs, then of course they refused to go and demanded loads of money – so I had to go and command them to leave and threaten them with a bobby. Very busy unpacking and altering the Gemmell drawing-room, making it habitable. We had many tea-parties and went to lots of plays, also went several times to the Fisheries – the whole place beautifully lit with the electric light and thousands of Chinese lanterns.

July, 1883

The Abbey Lodge dance – lots of nice chaps – enjoyed ourselves very much – got home about four. On Sunday heard by far the loveliest anthem that ever was written to my mind – at St. Anne's, Soho, *Oh, for the Wings* – drank it in and it remained with me all day. Went to a tea-party at Cressie's [Cresswell Cresswell] to meet the great Oscar Wilde. He is grown enormously fat, with a huge face and tight curls all over his head – not at all the aesthetic he used to look. He was very amusing and talked cleverly, but it was all monologue and not conversation.

He is vulgar, I think, and lolls about in, I suppose, poetic attitudes with crumpled shirt cuffs turned back over his coat sleeves!

August, 1883

Back at Hunstanton. Walked along the cliffs to Old Hunstanton, meaning to bathe, not a soul about, but the tide miles out. Ran down in our suits and when we had left the shore a good way behind, had some wild dances, sand ballets – we two, two Skipwiths, three Fenwicks and Miss Piers – all with floating hair and blue and red suits. It was very good fun, but as to bathing, after wading nearly to Boston, with a mussel bed under foot, the water was just up to our knees!

September, 1883

We sisters go to Penshurst, the most lovely huge place built at different dates, some in 1370. The house is full of lovely pictures and treasures of art, also a small library of six thousand books and heaps of old china, silver and curiosities. Next day, walked in the garden with Lord de L'Isle and the rest, a garden full of cut yew hedges and old-fashioned flowers and ponds. I painted alone in the State Room one day – it was a public day and the British public simply poured in with creaky boots and muffled idiotic remarks, but presently a change and I had rather a romantic meeting – much to my surprise – with one Adrian Hope – a pal of Jo Joliffe's (who used to be a pal of mine years ago). He had come to see the house and garden with some friends, so we chatted and walked about – it was odd and pleasant.

December, 1883

Tom arrived, full of his London doings, he brought two most interesting things with him, a presentation sword given to 'Edward Troubridge Esq.' in 1805 (our grandfather), and a huge box of papers and letters of Papa's, *and* the original Nelson letters to our great grandfather [now at Greenwich Museum]. They have all been hidden away in a musty old lawyer's office in London. Tom met Uncle Charles (Gurney) in town who told him of them.

December 31st, 1883

Eleven-thirty, New Year's Eve – only half an hour left of poor old '83. We four – Amy, Laura, Vi and Helen – are sitting round the fire in our little house at Hunstanton – Tom is on his way to Ireland, and darling Ernest far away in South America. So we sit at home and think of them and drink their healths in mulled claret. The last day that is left me to write in this poor journal – I am very sorry – it has been such a nice, happy, prosperous year for all of us Troubridges. Adieu, Old Year – (It ended very industriously for us, for we were working hard at a Christmas Tree we give tomorrow to thirty-six poor children here) and so farewell.

1884

Very busy with my *Little Mermaid* drawings, working hard and steadily. Being rather hard up for something to do we chartered three tricycles and went a voyage into the country, ribaldly mounted on these most vulgar inventions. We tore along the most lonely lanes we could find, two of the horrible machines entirely refused to be guided, so the afternoon was not without excitement. Amy's ran violently up a bank and landed her in a heap by the roadside twice, amidst shouts of laughter from the rest of the *cortège*. I was the only one who really escaped a spill by jumping off and running to its head whenever my huge tricycle appeared rather restive. Discretion is ever so much better than valour – on tricycles anyhow!

Go to a local concert, Mrs. Whitty (the doctor's wife) in a scarlet satin ball-gown, with long scarlet silk gloves, murmured passionate love songs in a voice inaudible from fright, like a hen mourning into a feather bed. Four frightful men stood in a row and sang, in dull voices, with duller faces, *Kiss me – kiss me* for about half an hour. However, no one volunteered, so they had to subside. We nearly died of suppressed laughter.

March, 1884

Go to London, to stay in Thurloe Square, with Rosy and

Johnny Birkbeck. At the Grosvenor Gallery became immediately
absorbed in the lovely pictures, an exhibition entirely of Sir
Joshua Reynolds' paintings (to close tonight – imagine my luck
in just managing to see them). Revelled in the lovely old world
faces. On March 28th heard of the sudden death of the Duke of
Albany, so on the 30th managed to turn out in mourning. Set off
en famille for St. Paul's Cathedral, went by underground – quick
and cheap – but very poisonous. I had not been to St. Paul's since
I was quite a child, and I was much impressed by it. There was a
vast multitude of mourning people (over six thousand), and in
the middle of the service they played the Dead March in *Saul*. I
shall never forget it as long as I live, it was grand on that magnificent organ, the peals of thunder and then the air wailing
forth, first loud then like a far away echo. It was unutterably
melancholy and thrilled me through and through.

April, 1884

To Yarmouth with Lancer, to the ancient Toll House to see a
relic of our great grandfather [Admiral Sir Thomas Troubridge],
a chair in the shape of a boat in which he was chaired round the
town when he was member for Yarmouth in 1802.

At Keswick. While sleeping the sleep of the just there was
actually an *earthquake*, the first for years in England. Most people
in the house felt it, but slightly. It did a lot of damage in some
parts. Received a letter from the Gemmells closing with our offer
of exchanging houses again, and congrats on Ernest's appointment to the Royal Yacht.

June, 1884

Staying at Abbey Lodge. With Marie [de Bunsen] to the
Westminster Palace Hotel to see Irving Bishop, the thought
reader, who gave a wonderful performance – deeply interesting
and awfully amusing too. All the representatives of the Press were
there, taking notes. He did some extraordinary and perfectly
inexplicable things, and was successful in three experiments out
of four.

To Sandown, not very many people and few we knew, but the whole thing was amusing, the lawn and garden so pretty and the Guards' Band playing all day. The fact is, after Hunstanton *anything* and *everything* is amusing! I love seeing the horses sweep past and the excitement of the whole thing.

The longest day – June 21st – and we were thankful for it, for it was none too long for all we had to do (the great move to Gloucester Street). We had a nice journey, not too hot, at least as nice as a train journey can be, which is not saying much. Arrived at Liverpool Street, found the two omnibuses in readiness, lots of horrible dirty roughs followed to help with the luggage, but fortunately we had remembered last year and had engaged beforehand a respectable huge man who kept all the others at bay for us.

Met Violet Cochrane Baillie, who asked us to go and call on Maria Scott. We went to see her in Sloane Street – such a funny old thing, a double widow of seventy, wearing a golden wig! She was a first cousin of Papa's and we had never seen her since old days. She was amusing and clever to talk to, giving us her views on matrimony and blaming everyone all round for enjoying their single-blessedness!

June 26th, an ever-to-be-remembered day, a delightful Gold Letter day in our family history – at ten o'clock in the morning who should walk calmly into the drawing-room, all sun-burnt and heavenly-looking, but darling Ernest straight from South America. He had started the day after he read of his appointment and had been five weeks on the road. Resisting loads of invitations to stay in Paris he came straight on to us and by the merest piece of luck heard we were here, or he would have gone flying off to Hunstanton. All quite demoralised all day and could do nothing but laugh and talk together and pinch him to see if he was real.

To Monkham's in the afternoon, a lovely day – almost too hot, a huge strawberry and hay and Corney Grain party turned on. Rather enjoyed it – heard Corney Grain who was perfectly killing. We were introduced to him and travelled back to London together, which was rather fun.

July, 1884

Mr. and Mrs. Oscar Wilde to tea, she dressed for the part in drimp white muslin, with absolutely *no* bustle, saffron coloured silk swathed about her shoulders, a huge cartwheel Gainsborough hat, white and bright yellow stockings and shoes – she looked too hopeless and we thought her shy and dull – he was amusing of course.

Went with a not very exciting party to the Healtheries Exhibition at the Horticultural Gardens [then in Queen's Gate] and thought it awfully flat. However, as we were buying chocolates at the most delicious place, Mr. Joliffe and Mr. Hope appeared. They had been chasing us all over the exhibition, so off we went *à quatre*, as it was impossible to remain in a bunch in such a crowd. Mr. Hope and I went and drank milk and ate brown biscuits at the Dairy. (I was rather agreeably surprised – as I thought him so very smart and Londony – that he liked drinking milk!) When he and Jo Joliffe were looking for us Mr. Hope had suggested that we would be at some highbrow part of the Exhibition – looking at pictures I think, but Jo had said firmly, 'If I know the Troubridges they will be at the Chocolate Stall', and we were!

Feeling very happy went to Henley for the day, and again Mr. Hope was of the party, though Jo was there too so I had to divide my attentions. Met again in the Park on Sunday, when Mr. Hope and Jo sheltered me from the rain under a tree. Jo had to return to the Bachelors Club [he was the Secretary], but Mr. Hope escorted me to lunch in Belgrave Square and later met me at Abbey Lodge, where we sat and talked in the garden for a long time and walked part of the way back to Gloucester Street together.

He came to tea on the 8th, returned to dine and do a play, and on to supper at the Salisbury Club. Met in the park on the 9th, we lunched at Gloucester Street on the 10th and to the Healtheries afterwards – with others – but we two roamed about *à deux* and enjoyed ourselves. Back to tea at G. St. when Mr. Hope stayed till nearly eight. Then we thought of doing a play, so we dined and went a party to the New Empire, and Mr. Hope gave us all supper at the Salisbury.

Two days – with no meetings. On the 13th met in the Park and settled to go to the Zoo in the afternoon, I had to drive there in a hansom with Jo, but drove back with Mr. Hope. Went to a ball on the 14th, and enjoyed it immensely, dancing till the sun was shining, and *all* my friends were there. To a theatre party on the 15th and supper after, then Mr. Hope brought me home. July 17th – a letter that pleased me very much was put into my hand this morning when I woke – and a basket of roses from Adrian Hope. He arrived at four and brought me two beautiful stuffed peacocks from Ceylon – one he had shot there and the other had been his tame peacock, and ill luck or not they gave me great pleasure.

After some blank days I had to write one note that took me some little time ... On the 22nd had a tea-party and Mr. Hope came and stayed very late, and we sat on the balcony and talked. On the 23rd we all dined with Lord and Lady Wallscourt and went on to a Fête at the Healtheries where we had the most delightful evening – lost our party directly and wandered about together listening to the lovely music, the whole place was made into a sort of Fairyland for the Fête night – I felt very happy – Mr. Hope and I sat together in a quiet corner and had a long talk and later we went to 'Ceylon' for coffee. I shall always remember this evening – Mr. H. took me home about one o'clock. He came to tea on the 24th, and after dinner went, in a large party, to Madame Tussaud's and felt like country cousins, gloating over the Horrors.

On the 26th we all met at the theatre (to see Sarah Bernhardt in *Adrienne Lecouvreur*) and went on to supper with Mr. Hope at the Salisbury. He is a very good host and the whole thing was amusing – a lovely bouquet of carnations for each of us. (Mine was the loveliest!) On the 28th had a tea-party, and Tom brought Mr. Hope with him – last but not least – he stayed late after everyone else, having done a great deal of duty and helped us through our unusually elderly tea-party. He did not go till we

had arranged a little party for this evening – a 'Drum' with
Cressie as chaperon, and the glorious little plan came off most
successfully – beginning early and ending early – next morning!
On the 29th we went, a large party, to the Empire and on to
supper with Jo at the Bachelors. After supper we spent the evening in Jo's little red drawing-room, when A.H. and I sat in the
window and *astronomised* till two o'clock in the morning . . .

On the 30th we all went to the New Club Ball. We two had a
very happy time and soared above all pin-pricks (Amy and Tom
being furious with various people) – with such a floor, such
music, and such a partner – home around three-thirty! On the
31st, to Goodwood with Jo, Mrs. Yorke Bevan and Mr. Hope.
The day is a very mixed one to look back on – crowds of people
and the whole thing a very pretty sight, but the party would not
sort itself aright and Mr. Hope and I were a prey to the unremit-
ting attentions of Mrs. Bevan and Jo, and nothing short of down-
right rudeness could have rescued us from their clutches. We
missed the 'special' by five minutes, and had a long wait for
another train. A long journey home, tired but happy, talking in
a corner with A.H. while Jo slept and Mrs. Bevan sulked! On
August 1st he came to tea and we two sat on the balcony and
talked till past eight – and I thought no time had ever flown so
fast.

August 2nd, 1884 – THE DAY OF MY LIFE
 . . . but quite unconscious of it, I rose, breakfasted, talked and
laughed as on any ordinary day, and afterwards, feeling rather in
a fright I went off all by myself to interview a strange Mr. Cooper
about my book. He turned out to be a most harmless civil old
chap, who having had a letter from Caldecott praising my drawings is anxious to do what he can about them.

A lovely day, a day to spend lying in a wood amongst ferns
and flowers. Home to lunch and afterwards, about four, drove
with Amy to the Grosvenor Gallery. Mr. Hope met us there and
Jack St. Aubyn. Looked at the pictures together and spent a
quiet time. Then Vi joined us and we all went to Charbonnel

next door – for iced coffees and *petits fours*. It *was* a hot day. Walked partly home and said 'au revoir', not good-bye.

Alone to dinner, we three – wore my black frock with some red carnations. Amy dressed up the strangest and most fantastic dummy and called it 'Aunt Chatty' – to preside at the Drum as sundry cousins had failed. Mr. St. Leger came and was funny, but I was not in tune with fooling and remained on the balcony, where there was a rising moon, until Adrian came very late. I had faithfully promised to play games with the others and not spend a tête-à-tête evening – but all such promises were thrown to the winds – we only came in and danced for a few minutes with the rest, and then sat there together all the evening, and when the moon had risen above the housetops and looked down on us – we knew that we loved each other – till Death us do part – and were very happy.

I still call him 'Mr. Hope' but I am trying to get used to the other in my mind. On August 8th Adrian came to take me to the station, for Tom [who was in the 60th] was stationed at Limerick and he and a group of his brother officers had taken a house at Knocklofty near Clonmel, for the fishing and we four sisters were invited to keep house for them. We drove off together, waving good-bye to Gloucester Street – such a drive – almost too happy to feel how near the parting was. As we passed the Abbey he put on my finger the most lovely sapphire ring. Our horse fell down but we scarcely noticed it. Arrived at Euston he took care of us all, but the train went dreadfully soon and we had to say our first good-bye – though we called it 'au revoir'.

August 9th

Arrived at Clonmel and had an amusing drive to Knocklofty, all four of us clinging to an outside car with a splendid Irish driver. Thought the house delightful. On August 16th Adrian arrived – no difficulty about staying at the hotel at Knocklofty – it did not exist! A good Irishman, our next door neighbour, had asked Mr. Hope to stay at Marlfield, though he only met him on the train by chance coming from Dublin. After dinner Amy sang to us till Adrian had to go – at half past ten! I saw him off for his lonely walk, with a lantern and in his pocket a loaded pistol in case of 'Moonrakers' [wild Irish Agrarian disturbances].

After the announcement of our engagement had appeared in the *Morning Post* it was considered all right for Adrian to stay in the house with us. When Tanner, our faithful maid, unpacked for him, she shed salt tears all over his shirts, saying, 'If only it hadn't been Miss Laura!' The weather was perfect (I suppose the keen fishermen must have grumbled), but we were divinely happy, in fact it was the happiest time of my life.

October 2nd – last day at Knocklofty – all the days have been happy days – I have been too happy to write of our doings, for words are too dull and cold to describe it all – at least the words that I could write here – in this book where any eye may read what I write. But they will not be forgotten – Adrian and I will keep the memory of them in our hearts for ever. *The happiest brightest summer that we shall ever know* [the refrain of one of this year's popular songs] for we have never been so happy in our lives, whatever the future may have in store for us.

Later in October Adrian came on a sort of tour of my relations, to make their acquaintance, and all the cousins made him very welcome – and he won all hearts, also making friends with Lawrence Jones – my ex-admirer. We ended up at the 'Castle' in Hunstanton, which he loved. On November 4th Adrian had to return to London. After he had left, feeling very sad, I had down a big box of letters and burned some I had been meaning to destroy – read them all over first – and had not a regret in the world!

December, 1884

Very busy rehearsing *Sweethearts* again, for some performances at West Newton, got up by the Chapmans – not with Douglas Grant as he was abroad, but with a Mr. Lambert. Adrian joined us at Runcton on the 23rd, when we had a merry time and danced on Christmas night, and had a dance with an impromptu *Cotillon* on Boxing night.

On the 29th, go on to the Chapmans at Hillington. Adrian sees the dress rehearsal. The play went off well, but I felt nervous – A. was there in the front row – I could not help seeing him, but he liked *Sweethearts* very much, and we sat together afterwards to see *The Comical Countess*. The next day, an enormous audience, the Sandringham party were very punctual and seemed to like the play. The Prince and Princess and all their children were there, and a large party staying in the house. I did not feel nervous that night, and I think the play went very well. Afterwards the Prince came and talked to me, paid me compliments about my acting and said he had enjoyed it. I think I felt rather pleased, but I missed Adrian horribly.

December 31st, 1884

So the day dwindled and faded away – the last day of the year – but all my brightest thoughts seem for the future now, and I scarcely thought of the dying year except for the happiness it has brought us. Yet another performance at West Newton – home about ten – had an amusing supper, all drank healths, afterwards played games and rather romped till nearly twelve, but my own thoughts were all of A., though I felt rather happy and laughed and played with the rest.

At twelve we all went to the hall and opened the door to let the New Year in. It was a lovely still night, with a bright moon and very frosty. We all ran out into the garden to welcome 1885 and wished each other a Happy New Year all round. I felt so funny with my powdered hair and my white frock – the first and second acts of *Sweethearts* blended – but in my life it is only the first that we have played yet – and even that is not finished.

The First Royal Portraits 1892

On January 2nd, 1892 I went down for the first time in my life to stay at Quarr Abbey in the Isle of Wight with my great aunt Lady Cochrane, taking my daughter Jaqueline (who was not yet three) and Nana Hendry. I felt it would be for long, and so it turned out. The object of my visit was to do the portrait in pastels of Minnie [Minnie Cochrane, Lady-in-waiting to Princess Beatrice of Battenberg], who with her quaint grey curly hair, pink cheeks and bright pretty face is a perfect subject.

But it was painting under difficulties. The first day I set to work and made some sketches from Minnie but only had about an hour as at twelve she had to go off to lunch at Osborne (Queen Victoria's residence) and did not get back till after dark. However I did what I could without her and tried to possess my soul in patience. The next day, January 5th, set to work and hoped for a quiet morning at my picture, but just when we were settled the Princess arrived so off Minnie had to go for a good half-hour. Once more at work when another ring was heard, this time it was the Doctor to see Min. He stayed an age, and so by lunch I seemed scarcely started, and afterwards Minnie had to go to Ryde to get things for her Princess (Beatrice), and back at dark. January 6th, again Minnie had to go to lunch at Osborne, and desert me after an hour's sitting, but I could get on with the background and am beginning to see the picture. The next day, a good morning's work, and the picture really making way. People to lunch, so no more sittings from Minnie, but I worked on at the background and dress.

January 9th, at work all day to get the picture finished and framed, ready to go to Osborne first thing tomorrow. The Queen wished the picture to be sent over with others of my drawings besides – the Mermaid designs, the Cupid autotypes, Cyril Wilde's portrait etc.

The gossip from Osborne is rather fun – I could make a small fortune from writing low paragraphs for *Modern Society*! Min is to take part in the Tableaux Vivants next week. Alick Yorke (a gentleman-in-waiting to Queen Victoria) is Stage Manager and fusses about them to any extent. By the Queen's special wish Minnie is cast for the two parts she seems least suited for in the whole world, first an Indian woman – Minnie with her grey-white hair and pink cheeks, secondly – Rebecca at the Well in Bible times, with an Indian man as Isaac, peering into a large earthenware pot which Rebecca is to hold, and looking, Minnie says, exactly like a Sanitary Inspector!

A telegram came inviting Adrian (who was coming to stay for a few days) and me to the evening party at Osborne with the Tableaux Vivants, and afterwards to a sort of Drawing Room. I was presented to Her Majesty there and made my lowest curtsy. She said to me, 'Mrs. Hope, I have so much admired your beautiful drawings.' It was rather like a dream I thought. A supper followed, and a nice sailor off the Royal Yacht, and a great friend of Ernest's, took me in. It was a gay scene.

When I got back from painting the two little Legge children at Kent House I found a message to say that the Queen liked my pastels so much she wished me to do portraits of the Connaught children, Princess Beatrice and her little girl Princess Ena [later Queen of Spain] – felt keen about it but rather overwhelmed. It was Cyril Wilde's picture that made them so keen about Princess Ena who, they say, is very pretty. She is to be done in the same style, as they all liked it so much.

Then came the news of the death of the poor young Duke of Clarence, who was so soon to be married. In spite of this tragedy I found I was still expected at the Castle, and so on January 14th I began to do the portraits for the Queen.

Osborne seemed so full of mourners. It could scarcely be realised by the nation, indeed in my life I never remember any thing so stirring to the feelings of the whole country, but of course it will not make a lasting impression as there is no personal loss to the country in the Duke's death – he being a young knight with his spurs to win – but the sorrow and sympathy for his family and for Princess May was very widespread. Being at Osborne at the time made it all very real to me. Adrian had to go back to our lonely little home, and I stayed on to do these commissions for the Queen, and a long, long work it turned out.

As each one was finished, a fresh task was found for me. As an episode in one's life it was unique, as a start as a portrait painter it was excellent, but it needed all my courage and endurance to carry through all this work every day and the whole day for several weeks. My days were all alike, first a six-mile drive from Quarr to Osborne – the weather cruelly cold, sometimes the Princess sent her Hungarian carriage with the curious black leather curtains for me, but more often I went in Lady Cochrane's brougham, and such a long six miles it seemed, with many steep hills.

A room in Princess Beatrice's wing was turned into my studio as it had a north light. At all hours and any hours the Royalties came and went, in and out of the studio, and often remained to watch me at work – most trying it was, in spite of their kindness and friendliness, and also the fact that they were pleased with my portraits.

At two o'clock I went, weary and still in my work in mind, to rather formidable luncheons with the Household – many of whom I knew and they were most friendly. Still, I was really too fatigued to enjoy such functions. After lunch I flew back to my work and remained till dark – three-thirty or four o'clock, and then unless I stayed to tea in the ladies' drawing-room (which I sometimes did) I went my long and weary drive, up hill and down dale, until at last the lights of Quarr gleamed upon my tired eyes, and there was tea and Jaqueline to welcome me.

When I first started my sittings with the little Princesses I had rather a lot of visitors – Princess Louise and Lord Lorne, Princess Christian, Princess Victoria, the Duke and Duchess of Connaught and Prince Henry of Battenberg all came in to see what I was about. I seemed to be making bobs all day long! They all looked so sad, and all of course in deep black – the Queen had five hundred telegrams of sympathy in one day. Prince Eddy's death seems to make no difference to my work, indeed I think my pastels are a sort of distraction to them all. I soon felt less nervous, and set to work at the little Princesses, who sat in turn. They were dressed as acolytes, as they had appeared in one of the Tableaux, with all their pretty long fair hair bundled up under little round red caps. I made a good start, but it was rather trying when the Duke came and sat on a box at my elbow, watching every stroke. In fact I worked most of the time with the Duke almost leaning on my arm! Presently Princess Beatrice came and stood on the other side, and the rest of the royalties kept popping in and out all the time – Princess Louise making some very good suggestions. (She made a clever sketch for the background which I copied.)

After the little Princesses I made some sketches for Prince Arthur's portrait and began it. This was a life-size head, the little boy was a restless sitter but very amiable. He used to entertain me by saying, 'You know, Mrs. Hope, in India there are snakes.' [The Connaughts had just returned from the East]. Then would follow a little anecdote about snakes, or, 'You know, Mrs. Hope, in India there are black people,' and then another anecdote.

On January 19th all the Royalties except Princess Louise went up to Buckingham Palace for the funeral. I enjoyed my quiet day's work, free from interruptions, and got on with my pictures. A few days later the Duchess of Connaught came to say good-bye and made me a nice little speech of thanks and said she would always value the pictures. She was shy which made her seem stiff, but the Duke was charming, his friendly simplicity was a great contrast to Prince Henry of Battenberg, who used to come into the studio, click his heels and make a very stiff bow.

The following Sunday Princess Beatrice, Princess Ena, Prince Henry and Lord Lorne drove over to Quarr in the afternoon. Jaqueline was sent for and amused everyone by her quaint remarks. She arrived panting, along the passage, saying in a sort of chant, 'Here I come, here I come,' then took two chairs and dragged them into the middle of the room, took Princess Ena by the hand and said, 'Princess *Eno*, come and sit alongside of me.'

Then, looking at her hands she said, admiringly, 'What lovely gloves *you've* got – kid! I've only got old shabby woolly ones – but I have got some others.' Having only just come in she pulled off a glove and held it up in disgust, to everyone's amusement, and Princess Beatrice said, 'Ena has woollen ones too for the garden.'

The next day went off early to Osborne with little Jaqueline, all in white like a snowball – Hendry too of course – as they had been invited for the day. They thoroughly enjoyed their visit and tiny Jaqueline was made much of. She went for a toddle, hand-in-hand with Prince Leopold and six-year-old Prince Drino (as they call the eldest boy). The two little fellows were quarrelling as to which should walk with her, so to keep the peace she had to give a hand to each.

A squad of nurses and a little tiny open carriage, a miniature Victoria drawn by a white donkey and led by a footman, went with Prince Leopold and Prince Drino. So when Jaqueline was tired she drove with the little Princes, and alone part of the time as they wished to lead the donkey and open the gates for her – and as she passed they made her low bows and pretended she was the Queen!

Jaqueline was equal to the occasion and longed to stay at Osborne. Princess Beatrice was very taken with her. The only fiasco was after lunch, when the children all went down to see the Queen. Princess Beatrice told me she particularly wished the Queen to see Jaqueline as she was so sweet and not at all shy. So she went down with the little Princes to the Queen's dining-room, led by the two boys and was quite happy until she suddenly saw three huge Indian servants behind the Queen's chair, when she fled from the room! She did not cry but just bolted, and nothing would induce her to come into the room again.

I began the portrait of little Princess Ena, who is fair and pretty. At one of the sittings I was left quite alone with her for a few minutes and she took the opportunity to say, 'I do *squeak* when they curl my hair – and now *you* are here they curl it *three* times a day!'

After her I made a pencil sketch of Princess Beatrice which was approved of, and made a beginning of the portrait. It will be rather difficult I foresee and Prince Henry, who is sternly realistic and rather trying, will wander round urging me to make her cheeks larger and her waist shorter – when I would fain idealise her proportions. He would stand beside me, making a long telescope with his hands, saying, 'Yes, Mrs. Hope, yes – but the Princess is larger.' To which I would answer, 'Very well, Sir,' and add flowing curves. But the moment he went out of the room the poor Princess would jump up and come round to the easel, saying 'Oh, Mrs. Hope, not so large please!' and I would answer, 'Very well, Ma'am,' and reduce the curves! I am glad he goes tomorrow.

On February 7 the Queen had a Cabinet Council, but first she had an audience with Jaqueline! A messenger came to the studio to say Her Majesty wished to see Miss Hope, so Princess Beatrice took her off to the Queen's sitting-room and Hendry went to the door and waited outside. (I am told the Queen was so kind she ordered all the Indian servants to keep out of sight so that she should not be frightened this time.) The Queen was delighted with Baby – she kissed her and asked her name. Baby said, 'Jaqueline Louise Rachel Hope.' Hendry could hear this, then the door was shut, but she could hear them talking and laughing. The Queen herself told me that she had asked Jaqueline where she was staying, adding, 'I don't know why I asked a baby such a question, but she answered so prettily – "I am staying at Quarr with dear Lady C."' Her Majesty seemed very amused at this. (Later on my brother Tom used to tell a story that the Queen also asked Jaqueline where she lived – which of course she may have done – and that she answered, 'In Brompton Road, opposite Harrods.' I believe this appeared in some newspaper and that Harrods wanted to use it as an advertisement!) As it was wet in the afternoon all the children played in the corridor. Jaqueline was not the least shy and played at horses and at ball and talked with them all. When she left Prince Drino gave her a toy soldier as a souvenir, 'to be kept for ever'.*

The Princess of Wales and the two Princesses came to see me and stayed a long time in my studio, looking at everything and talking of Ernest and Norfolk etc. They were so nice, but the Princess's face is so wan and pathetic, it quite haunts me. I also had a long visit from Prince George, he was very nice and talked much of Ernest. His sisters had told me the day before, 'We often hear of your brother, he is George's best friend.'

Princess Beatrice is difficult to paint, there is no doubt. I said so to Sir Henry Ponsonby [Queen Victoria's Private Secretary] at lunch when I was sitting next to him. I put it neatly, that her face changed so, but he was not so courtly and said at once, 'Yes, she is stolid – no expression at all when she is still. Tell her Prince Henry has been seen flirting with the Spanish ladies (he had gone to Gibraltar) – that will call up an expression!' I laughed and said I thought it might give her rather too much animation.

The Princess often sends her little cart for me. I like it because we fly along, tearing up all the hills and do the six miles to Quarr in just under the half-hour. I had a long tête-à-tête with Princess Beatrice yesterday and she asked me to spend the day at Windsor Castle before they go abroad, 'to see the pictures'. I hope it will not be forgotten.

I had a long visit from the Queen herself. She had not been to the studio before, though the pictures are often taken off to be shown to her. She was so very nice and kind – quite an old dear. She liked the picture of Princess Beatrice, made a few good helpful remarks and chaffed about the Princess making a face while she is sitting. The Queen's criticisms were very gently made, as she said almost apologetically, 'You see I know Bee's face so well.'

It would be an awful pity not to follow up the success that has fallen on me here in this surprising way. Minnie said the Queen would put it in the Court Circular later, about my doing these

* [I have it still.]

portraits, and meanwhile advised us to tell all our friends, as the more it was known the better – and my prices of course will go up. I shall have made over £90 in these two months – but it has been a strain, not so much the actual work as the conditions, which are so fatiguing, and I long for the freedom and peace of my own studio.

I think that except the Edinburghs, I saw all the Royal Family while I was there. It was an odd experience altogether, and it came to an abrupt end. All the time I had had a haunting fear that Adrian would or might be ill, and at last it was so. He had a very bad attack of influenza, the third within eighteen months.

No letters from him for three days gave me sleepless nights, then I wired, and got the answer from the doctor, saying his temperature was 102 degrees. I showed it to Princess Beatrice, whose second portrait I had begun, and she arranged for me to leave at once. So, saying good-bye to all my friends at Osborne, I drove over that long road for the last time.

The Cochranes, who had been so kind and made us as welcome as possible all this long visit, then helped me to collect all our things and the next morning early we said many goodbyes and in a terrible snow storm and gale started for home. My anxiety for Adrian was intense and I did not even think of the wild weather.

Oh, the joy of being united again. Softly I sped upstairs, very gently opened the bedroom door, and there was my Adrian, lying in bed – just faintly smiling as he looked with loving eyes at me. He could only hold my hand, he was too weak to talk. Then I found how very ill he had been, with influenza and bronchitis, too, and most thankful I felt that I had found it out and returned.

Some Family History

On my mother's side we had relations enough, but on my father's a most meagre allowance. Besides my grandmother we only had one unmarried aunt – Charlotte [Chatty] – and four Walrond first cousins, with very few more distantly related, and no one of the name.

My paternal grandmother, Lady (Anna Maria) Troubridge, was the eldest daughter of Admiral the Hon. Sir Alexander Cochrane, G.C.B., sixth son of the 8th Earl of Dundonald, and Maria Shaw, daughter of David Shaw of New York. Maria Shaw had first married Captain Sir Jacob Wheate, R.N., who sailed with the British Fleet into New York harbour and captured the fair American, then aged only fifteen. Three months later he died, and his young widow returned to her own people. But she happily found another sailor lover in my great grandfather (Sir Alexander Cochrane), who had already met and admired 'the fair Maria'. On returning from a short cruise, and finding her a widow, he quickly carried off the prize. They lived abroad a great deal as, when Admiral, he held several appointments in distant lands. Her descendants with whom we have the strongest ties of friendship are Louisa and Minnie Cochrane, daughters of her eldest son, Admiral Sir Thomas Cochrane.

My grandfather, Sir Edward Thomas Troubridge (afterwards one of the Lords of the Admiralty, and M.P. for Sandwich), succeeded his father – Admiral Sir Thomas Troubridge (one of Nelson's Captains) in 1809, two years after his father was assumed to have been lost at sea in his flag ship, the *Blenheim*, on his voyage from the East Indies to take up a command at the Cape. (James Montgomerie wrote a melancholy poem on this subject, beginning *He sought his sire from shore to shore – But sought his sire in vain*, with many verses in the same spirit. The poets of that age revelled in tragedy, when not babbling of green fields.) Sir Thomas (my great grandfather) had married a widow, Mrs. Frances Richardson, née Northall, with daughters and sons. She died in 1798, leaving one Troubridge daughter, Charlotte (afterwards Lady Grey Egerton), and one son, Sir Edward Thomas, my grandfather.

The first mention of the Cochranes meeting the Troubridge family occurs in a letter in 1809 from Anna Maria Cochrane (later my grandmother) to her father, Sir Alexander, who was then Admiral at Bermuda.

No. 12 Portman Square.   *9th Sept. 1809*

   My dearest Father,

   Two days ago I received your note of the 26th of July and am grieved that you should suppose I would regret leaving Bath and masquerades etc. to go to you. That was never my reason. I have no doubt but that you are much Gayer than we have ever been – and as for Beaux, Never was a House where so few decent-looking ones are admitted. Uncle Basil has no idea of inviting any but Old Fogies. (Do not tell him my account of his Company). I was afraid that if you had your 'delightful family' in the West Indies it would most likely make you remain there longer than you otherwise would, but since I find it is quite the reverse, Believe me, I am perfectly ready and anxious to set off whenever an opportunity offers. I should prefer going with Tom [her brother] or Lord Cochrane [her cousin] to any other I know – even to Sir Thomas [Troubridge], who I hear you think I am to be married to! My beloved Father, do you think that Mama or I would have kept you so long in the Dark, if there had been any likelihood of such a thing taking place? I think him an Amiable pleasant young man – but that is not to say that 'he Loo's me – or I Loo' him.' You must not believe what you hear from Uncle – at least not all. We know that when he has no news he likes to make some. I do not think he ever saw us together. At present the Baronet is Flirting and Dancing away with the Ladies in Edinburgh – so that does not look as if he were desperate and as for me,

I am as lively, and more so I think, than when he was here. I do not think I am of as Gloomy a disposition as formerly, though I do not like talking a great deal, I have no objection to a little merriment now and then, and in whose Society could I be more happy than in yours? None I think.

I trust we shall soon meet and never separate for so long a time.

In spite of this filial and pious wish Anna Maria Cochrane did not go out to join her father in Bermuda, but was married to young Sir Thomas Troubridge in the autumn of 1810. My father, Thomas Hope St. Vincent, their eldest child, was born in London in May 1815, Edward Norwich – their second son – in Florence two years later. About this time my grandfather bought Rockville House, a pretty place near North Berwick, with fine views of the sea, rocks, and Berwick Law. There were visits to Stirling and Edinburgh for the balls (where there is a tradition that young Lady Troubridge even introduced the valse, so maligned of Byron). Then there were trips to London by the Leith Packet, taking six days to do the voyage, with 'contrary winds' like St. Paul; the travellers *returning* by post chaise, spending another week on the journey.

These visits to London were quite gay, they had many friends and relations there. Grandmama describes operas and dances, wearing pretty clothes – laced jackets for the Epsom Races are mentioned, where they picnicked, drank French wines, and won and lost some bets. There were visits to the Panorama, to Flirts Bazaar (whatever it may have been). There were card parties too, alluded to quite calmly in these tell-tale diaries.

Grandmama as we knew her gave no glimpse of past frivolities and the old diaries were safely locked away in the vast trunks and cupboards of that gloomy house in Bayswater where she lived and had her being in our youth. Of Tom Hope, as they called their eldest son (my father), and Edward Norwich, his brother, there are miniatures as merry little boys in tartan frocks with sporrans, standing at ease in pointed-toed patent leather shoes and very white socks, the Grampians frowning in the distance.

Two tiny scarlet cloth hunting coats of theirs still exist, absurdly small garments with gilt buttons stamped with a 'fox courant', as worn when *a-hunting we would go.*

Louisa Sophia, afterwards Mrs. Walrond, was their first daughter. Then came Robert Bruce, and Caroline. These two children died in their youth of some sort of decline. They were taken to Brighton to revive them, the scene of the one solitary story that has survived of Robert's short life. Queen Victoria, as a young girl, was walking on the beach with her ladies, when her shoe – probably a small satin sandal, became unfastened. Robert, who was quite a little fellow was playing by the sea and came gallantly to kneel at her feet and re-tie the ribbons, for which Princess Victoria smiled her thanks.

Many doctors were consulted for these dear children, but they died. Alexander Murray Cochrane, a lovely child of four, died in London about 1823. We have a pretty miniature of him, holding a dove in his arms, with blue eyes, dark curly hair and a smiling angel face. Charlotte Frances, their youngest child, although always thought delicate, survived them all by many years, and became our Aunt Chatty.

The wonder really seems to be that so many children did survive in those days of drastic treatment and want of hygiene, endless doses of brimstone and treacle and other violent remedies. Even sea bathing, such a joy to children nowadays, was rendered hideous by the presence of behemoth-like bathing women and men whose prey the children became, to be relentlessly ducked in deep water. Grandmama added to this a little idea of her own (told me by my father) that any child who desired to bathe must first drink a glass of salt water. A tumbler was always taken down to the beach with them and filled to the brim in the waves for this ordeal. As if children did not swallow enough and to spare when bathing, this addition must surely have been an emetic!

Another curious moral effort of my grandmother's was to prepare the infant mind to endure disappointments by telling her little girls of some party or delightful treat in store for them, allowing them to be dressed in their best for the occasion. Then, when ready and eagerly awaiting the carriage to bear them to the promised joys, Grandmama's cold voice would be heard, 'Louisa Sophia, Charlotte Frances, come back – retire to your rooms and remove your best dresses – there is no party!'

My father when young was always called by his second name, St. Vincent. He joined the Army early, as an Ensign, and afterwards was gazetted to the 7th Fusiliers, and was quartered first in Ireland and later in Canada, Malta, Gibraltar, and elsewhere abroad. At Gib. he distinguished himself by climbing the Rock at a place hitherto considered impregnable, and so not defended. After my father's exploit it was strongly fortified.

After my grandfather's death in 1852 my grandmother went to live with her two daughters at No. 72 Eaton Place. She became very anti-matrimonial at this time and instead of showing sympathy with her daughters wishing them to have nice homes of their own, she sternly repressed any kind of romance or love affair. Louisa and Chatty were both good-looking, especially Louisa, who had many admirers. One, to whom she was devoted, was suitable in every way, but was so ill-advised as to write and propose for her hand to her mother – who considered the poor lover too worldly-minded for the position. So she suppressed his letter and wrote him a curt note of refusal, giving this cruel letter to poor, guileless Louisa to hand herself to her lover coming out of church, Sunday being the day chosen for this base act. He, deeply hurt at what he naturally thought Louisa's heartless behaviour, left England at once. The poor girl, miserable, 'wore the willow' for him, losing her bright looks and gay spirits.

Not for years did she know how her mother had tricked her, and then she profited by this bitter experience by embarking on a secret engagement (and subsequent marriage) to an elderly clergyman, Mr. Theodore Walrond, a widower with two children.

Chatty, the youngest daughter, was what I have heard described as 'a spinster by nature', though she was both warm-hearted and sympathetic according to her views. If religion, of a peculiar kind, had not got hold of her so completely as it did she would have had more charm and allowed her merry wit to shine, but all was hidden under the canting language she loved, for both my aunt and grandmother became in time what they would call 'deeply religious' or 'earnest Christians'. Baptist Noel, Lord Gainsborough's brother, was a great personal friend of theirs, really their Pope, whose word was infallible. When he left the Church of England to become a Baptist minister they both joined his Chapel and modelled their lives entirely on ultra-Evangelical lines. In books telling of mid-Victorian days one's elders and betters were often alluded to as 'Olympians', that is a race apart whose existence and interests had barely any points of contact with one's own. When I think of my grandmother I realise hers was indeed a remote personality. As she died when I was still a child I can only write of her personally from a child's point of view. Had one known of her sorrows (she survived her husband and seven children) one might have felt more drawn to this infinitely remote being. Had she ever spoken to us of our dearly loved father and mother it would have been a link, but silence of the deepest enshrouded those who had gone, and even my father's portrait had the inevitable silk curtain drawn over it at that time.

This was due to the strange fashion of placing curtains, generally of green silk, over the portraits of those of the family who had died. I remember a new shroud of murky green merino was bought for a picture at our Runcton home, and a piece of this choice stuff being over, it was made into a dreadful frock for my little sister, Helen.

Index

INDEX

191